Riding Those MoodSwings

Rich Van Pelt

Helen Musick

David C. Cook Publishing Co.
Elgin, Illinois—Weston, Ontario

Custom Curriculum
Riding Those Mood Swings

Unless otherwise noted, Scripture quotations are from the Holy Bible, New International Version (NIV), © 1973, 1978, 1984 by International Bible Society. Used by permission of Zondervan Bible Publishers.

Published by David C. Cook Publishing Co.
850 North Grove Ave., Elgin, IL 60120
Cable address: DCCOOK
Series creator: John Duckworth
Series editor: Randy Southern
Editor: Randy Southern
Option writers: Sharon Stultz, Nelson E. Copeland, Jr., and Ellen Larson
Designer: Bill Paetzold
Cover illustrator: John Hayes
Inside illustrator: John Hayes
Printed in U.S.A.

ISBN: 0-7814-4998-7

CONTENTS

Sessions by Helen Musick
Options by Sharon Stultz, Nelson E. Copeland, Jr., and Ellen Larson

About the Authors

Helen Musick has over fifteen years of youth ministry experience. Currently she is a youth minister at First Alliance Church in Lexington, Kentucky. She also teaches youth ministry at Asbury Theological Seminary.

Sharon Stultz is a junior high editor in the Bible-in-Life division of David C. Cook. She is also a free-lance writer, and has worked extensively with junior highers.

Nelson E. Copeland, Jr. is a nationally known speaker and the author of several youth resources including *Great Games for City Kids* (Youth Specialties) and *A New Agenda for Urban Youth* (Winston-Derek). He is president of the Christian Education Coalition for African-American Leadership (CECAAL), an organization dedicated to reinforcing educational and cultural excellence among urban teenagers. He also serves as youth pastor at the First Baptist Church in Morton, Pennsylvania.

Ellen Larson is an educator and writer with degrees in education and theology. She has served as minister of Christian education in several churches, teaching teens and children, as well as their teachers. Her experience also includes teaching in public schools. She is the author of several books for Christian education teachers, and frequently leads training seminars for volunteer teachers. Ellen and her husband live in San Diego and are the parents of two daughters.

You've Made the Right Choice!

Thanks for choosing **Custom Curriculum**! We think your choice says at least three things about you:

(1) You know your group pretty well, and want your program to fit that group like a glove;

(2) You like having options instead of being boxed in by some far-off curriculum editor;

(3) You have a small mole on your left forearm, exactly two inches above the elbow.

OK, so we were wrong about the mole. But if you like having choices that help you tailor meetings to fit your kids, **Custom Curriculum** *is* the best place to be.

Going through Customs

In this (and every) **Custom Curriculum** volume, you'll find
• five great sessions you can use anytime, in any order.
• reproducible student handouts, at least one per session.
• a truckload of options for adapting the sessions to your group (more about that in a minute).
• a helpful get-you-ready article by a youth expert.
• clip art for making posters, fliers, and other kinds of publicity to get kids to your meetings.

Each **Custom Curriculum** session has three to six steps. No matter how many steps a session has, it's designed to achieve these goals:

• *Getting together.* Using an icebreaker activity, you'll help kids be glad they came to the meeting.

• *Getting thirsty.* Why should kids care about your topic? Why should they care what the Bible has to say about it? You'll want to take a few minutes to earn their interest before you start pouring the "living water."

• *Getting the Word.* By exploring and discussing carefully selected passages, you'll find out what God has to say.

• *Getting the point.* Here's where you'll help kids make the leap from principles to nitty-gritty situations they are likely to face.

• *Getting personal.* What should each group member do as a result of this session? You'll help each person find a specific "next-step" response that works for him or her.

Each session is written to last 45 to 60 minutes. But what if you have less time—or more? No problem! **Custom Curriculum** is all about … options!

What Are My Options?

Every **Custom Curriculum** session gives you fourteen kinds of options:

• *Extra Action*—for groups that learn better when they're physically moving (instead of just reading, writing, and discussing).

• *Combined Junior High/High School*—to use when you're mixing age levels, and an activity or case study would be too "young" or "old" for part of the group.

• *Small Group*—for adapting activities that would be tough with groups of fewer than eight kids.

• *Large Group*—to alter steps for groups of more than twenty kids.

• *Urban*—for fitting sessions to urban facilities and multiethnic (especially African-American) concerns.

• *Heard It All Before*—for fresh approaches that get past the defenses of kids who are jaded by years in church.

• *Little Bible Background*—to use when most of your kids are strangers to the Bible, or haven't made a Christian commitment.

• *Mostly Guys*—to focus on guys' interests and to substitute activities they might be more enthused about.

• *Mostly Girls*—to address girls' concerns and to substitute activities they might prefer.

• *Extra Fun*—for longer, more "rowdy" youth meetings where the emphasis is on fun.

• *Short Meeting Time*—tips for condensing the session to 30 minutes or so.

• *Fellowship & Worship*—for building deeper relationships or enabling kids to praise God together.

• *Media*—to spice up meetings with video, music, or other popular media.

• *Sixth Grade*—appearing only in junior high/middle school volumes, this option helps you change steps that sixth graders might find hard to understand or relate to.

• *Extra Challenge*—appearing only in high school volumes, this option lets you crank up the voltage for kids who are ready for more Scripture or more demanding personal application.

Each kind of option is offered twice in each session. So in this book, you get *almost 150* ways to tweak the meetings to fit your group!

Customizing a Session

All right, you may be thinking. *With all of these options flying around, how do I put a session together? I don't have a lot of time, you know.*

We know! That's why we've made **Custom Curriculum** as easy to follow as possible. Let's take a look at how you might prepare an actual meeting. You can do that in four easy steps:

(1) *Read the basic session plan.* Start by choosing one or more of the goals listed at the beginning of the session. You have three to pick from: a goal that emphasizes *knowledge,* one that stresses *understanding,* and one that emphasizes *action.* Choose one or more, depending on what *you* want to accomplish. Then read the basic plan to see what will work for you and what might not.

(2) *Choose your options.* You don't *have* to use any options at all; the

basic session plan would work well for many groups, and you may want to stick with it if you have absolutely no time to consider options. But if you want a more perfect fit, check out your choices.

As you read the basic session plan, you'll see small symbols in the margin. Each symbol stands for a different kind of option. When you see a symbol, it means that kind of option is offered for that step. Turn to the page noted by the symbol and you'll see that option explained.

Let's say you have a small group, mostly guys who get bored if they don't keep moving. You'll want to keep an eye out for three kinds of options: Small Group, Mostly Guys, and Extra Action. As you read the basic session, you might spot symbols that tell you there are Small Group options for Step 1 and Step 3—maybe a different way to play a game so that you don't need big teams, and a way to cover several Bible passages when just a few kids are looking them up. Then you see symbols telling you that there are Mostly Guys options for Step 2 and Step 4—perhaps a substitute activity that doesn't require too much self-disclosure, and a case study guys will relate to. Finally you see symbols indicating Extra Action options for Step 2 and Step 3—maybe an active way to get kids' opinions instead of handing out a survey, and a way to act out some verses instead of just looking them up.

After reading the options, you might decide to use four of them. You base your choices on your personal tastes and the traits of your group that you think are most important right now. **Custom Curriculum** offers you more options than you'll need, so you can pick your current favorites and plug others into future meetings if you like.

(3) *Use the checklist.* Once you've picked your options, keep track of them with the simple checklist that appears at the end of each option section (just before the start of the next session plan). This little form gives you a place to write down the materials you'll need too—since they depend on the options you've chosen.

(4) *Get your stuff together.* Gather your materials; photocopy any Repro Resources (reproducible student sheets) you've decided to use. And . . . you're ready!

The Custom Curriculum Challenge

Your kids are fortunate to have you as their leader. You see them not as a bunch of generic teenagers, but as real, live, unique kids. You care whether you really connect with them. That's why you're willing to take a few extra minutes to tailor your meetings to fit.

It's a challenge to work with real, live kids, isn't it? We think you deserve a standing ovation for taking that challenge. And we pray that **Custom Curriculum** helps you shape sessions that shape lives for Jesus Christ and His kingdom.

—*The Editors*

Talking with Junior Highers about Up-and-Down Feelings

by Rich Van Pelt

Skip was the stereotypical junior high guy. He could regularly be found bouncing off a wall or hanging from a chandelier. His energy and enthusiasm made him fun—but extremely exhausting—to be with. Skip's mom wondered whether it was possible for parents to survive their kids' adolescence.

One day I called to see if Skip was interested in going to the movies with a group of guys.

"Hey, Skip, how's it going?"

"Uh . . . OK, I guess."

"What's goin' on?"

"Not a whole lot . . ."

It wouldn't have taken Dick Tracy to discern that something was wrong. The tone of his voice was noticeably troubled. He spoke quietly and slowly. Something was up. I continued.

"Anything wrong?"

". . . Nah."

"You sure?"

"Well . . . she dumped me!"

After considerable hesitation, three simple words said it all: *"She dumped me!"* Skip was reeling from his first heartbreak. After three long months of building up the courage to ask Missy if they could "go out" and a few short weeks of adolescent bliss, Missy decided to "go out" with Skip's best friend. Skip was certain his world had come to an end.

The junior high years have been characterized as the "wonder years," but they weren't always wonderful. The physical, sexual, intellectual, psychological, and emotional changes of early adolescence require more of junior highers than the majority of them believe they have to give. In fact, at a time in their lives when most want nothing more than simply to be "normal," the only constant seems to be *change*. As a result, emotions appear supercharged. Everything is either the very best or the very worst. There doesn't seem to be an "in-between."

Which is where *we* enter the picture. Kids like Skip need adults in their lives who are willing to be with them in the up *and* the down times—adults who will take them seriously and help them understand that what they are experiencing is both normal and survivable. Let me offer a few suggestions on how we can be of assistance. What does it take to talk with junior highers about up and down feelings?

Focus on Building Relationships.

Several years ago, a major study was funded for the purpose of identifying the most effective curriculum for implementation in junior high schools nationwide. Survey results demonstrated that student-teacher relationship, not curriculum, is of paramount importance. Without quality student-teacher interaction, the best program or curriculum drowns in a sea of disinterest. Listen to a typical group of junior highers discuss their first week of school. Little attention is given to the subjects they will study, but major importance is placed on what teachers they will have. Kids respond to adults who like them and respect them. As trust develops, they will even risk sharing feelings.

Cultivate a Climate of Openness.

Don't naively assume that because the subject is "up-and-down feelings," kids in your group will feel safe enough to join in the discussion. Intentionally cultivate a climate where group members feel comfortable sharing from personal experience. Here are some ways to make that happen.

• Establish ground rules for the class or group.

(1) What is shared in the group stays in the group. Group members need assurance that anything they say will not be used against them! Unless kids believe that their opinions will be treated confidentially, they will be guarded in what they choose to share. As a result, little vulnerability will be exercised. In most cases, confidentiality should not be violated unless a student's life or the life of another is in jeopardy.

(2) Everyone has a right to speak—or remain silent. No one will be put on the spot. Each person may choose to share or to respectfully decline.

(3) No put-downs are allowed. It is imperative that the opinions of *all* be respected and protected. Group members inclined to discredit others will be invited to change—or leave.

(4) One person speaks at a time. Respect is non-negotiable. We communicate honor and value to each other by listening to what each other has to say.

(5) Everyone has equal status in the group. Personal value and the right to share has nothing to do with age, class, race, etc.

• Model transparency.

Leaders influence the tone of any group process. If honesty and transparency characterize our personal sharing, group members are more likely to follow suit. We've got to remember, however, that our goal is to talk as little as possible. In our role as facilitator, we work at drawing students into the discussion.

• Address real-life issues.

Up-and-down feelings are prompted by real-life issues. *Riding Those Mood Swings* honestly faces real issues that contribute to the feelings junior highers experience. Provide a place where they can freely explore and talk about any and all of those feelings.

Listen Empathetically.

Suicide is the second-leading cause of death among teenagers in America because too many of us believe that young people should be "seen and not heard." Statistics reveal that the average household in America with teenagers living in it spends 14.5 minutes a day communicating—with 12.5 of those minutes consumed by negative communication. The *average* teenager in America, therefore, can expect about 14 minutes a week of positive communication with mom and/or dad. Fourteen minutes a week of talking and listening is simply not enough. Youth workers, Sunday school teachers, and youth ministry volunteers must cultivate a climate in which kids feel safe enough to speak, and then take time to listen empathetically.

Someone once said, "Empathy is feeling your pain in my heart." For some time I've entertained a love-hate relationship with the TV series, *The Wonder Years.* Love, because the early episodes so accurately and poignantly portray life in junior high school, and *hate* for the same reason. I find it nearly impossible to watch an episode without being reminded of my own junior high experience—a time I, like many others, would rather forget. To be effective in ministry with junior highers and speak credibly with them about the realities of up-and-down feelings requires that we be willing to remember what it was like to be an early adolescent. When we remember how difficult those years and struggles were for us, we have greater capacity to genuinely come alongside kids on a gut level. There is a difference, however, between *empathy* and *arrogance.* Arrogance says, "I understand exactly what you are feeling," based solely on the premise that because I lived through a similar experience I can understand what you are going through. Empathy, by contrast, is coming alongside someone on a gut level, and taking the time to listen so that understanding may result.

Avoid "Adultisms."

Most adults remember a time in their childhood when they swore never to repeat something a parent said or did when they themselves bacame parents. For many, that commitment involved never hammering their children with phrases like:
- "You think *you* have it bad?"
- "Why don't you act your age?"
- "Just wait until you're a parent."
- "When I was your age . . ."
- "It's only puppy love."

We remember hating those messages because they seemed to discount what we were feeling. After all, puppy love is real to puppies! Noted child and adolescent psychologist Stephen Glenn says, "An adultism occurs any time an adult forgets what it is like to be a child and then expects, demands, and requires of the child who has never been an adult to think, act, understand, see and do things as an adult" (*Raising Self-Reliant Children in a Self-Indulgent World,* H. Stephen Glenn and Jane Nelsen, p. 91).

Offer Sound Biblical Advice.

Developmentally speaking, the early adolescent years represent a time of increased spiritual openness. Junior highers are eager to embrace the Christian faith, but they want to know how that faith relates to the real world in which they live. They need to know that the Christian faith is a faith of mountain tops *and* valleys, of highs *and* lows. They will be encouraged to learn that the God of the Bible meets people where they are—that great Bible characters like David, Job, Peter, and others struggled with feelings of loneliness, fear, anger, and abandonment. Junior highers should be encouraged that even in the worst of times, God offers peace and joy through His presence.

Know Your Limits.

These are tough times in which to be a kid. When given an opportunity to share about life's ups and downs, situations may surface that require specialized professional help. In an attempt to anesthetize their pain or lessen the demands of living, unprecedented numbers of young people are turning to high-risk activities like drinking or drugging, sexual promiscuity, eating disorders, and suicidal behavior. Learn to go with your gut. Whenever you sense that a young person's struggle is beyond your level of comfortability or training, seek professional assistance. Referral is a sign of strength, not weakness. Ask the advice of your supervisor or senior pastor, or contact a local mental health professional.

Rich Van Pelt is president of Alongside Ministries in Denver, Colorado. A twenty-five year veteran of youth ministry, Rich is the author of Intensive Care: Helping Kids in Crisis, *co-author of* The Compassion Project, *and a regular contributor to various youth ministry journals and perodicals. Rich is also a popular speaker at youth events, youth worker training conferences, and parent workshops nationwide.*

The images on these two pages are designed to help you promote this course within your church and community. Feel free to photocopy anything here and adapt it to fit your publicity needs. The stuff on this page could be used as a flier that you send or hand out to kids—or as a bulletin insert. The stuff on the next page could be used to add visual interest to newsletters, calendars, bulletin boards, or other promotions. Be creative and have fun!

Why Do Our Moods Change?

You know the feeling—one minute you're on top of the world, and not much later you're down in the dumps. For the next few weeks, we'll be looking at our up-and-down emotions in a new course called *Riding Those Mood Swings*. Hang on—it's going to be a wild ride.

Who:

When:

Where:

Questions? Call:

Riding Those Mood Swings

Riding Those Mood Swings

Come and see
what's cooking.

Is it wrong to be angry?

How do you try to cheer up?

Come and have a good/lousy time—
the choice is yours!

Why Do I Feel This Way?

YOUR GOALS FOR THIS SESSION:

Choose one or more

☐ To help kids recognize that emotions are a natural part of us—we were created with them.

☐ To help kids understand God's "emotions"—including His love, His anger, and His jealousy.

☐ To help kids choose a strategy for including God in their emotional lives.

☐ Other _____

Your Bible Base:

Genesis 1:27
Exodus 20:5
Numbers 32:13
Ecclesiastes 3:1-8
John 3:16

Emotions on Display

(Needed: Copies of Repro Resource 1)

As group members arrive, distribute copies of "A Trip to Grandmother's House" (Repro Resource 1). Assign the roles of the narrator, the young girl, the mother, the young man, and the stranger. (If you don't have many volunteers for the roles, you could double up on some of the parts.)

Explain that the actors will read the lines of the skit, while the rest of the group makes the noises called for in parentheses. Point out that a "cute sound" could be any sound people make when they see a cute baby or puppy dog ("awhhh," for instance). A "crying sound" could be anything from a sniffle to a bawling fit. A "yummy sound" could be any sound people make when they taste a food they like. "Boo, hiss" could be any sound members of an audience make when they don't like what they're seeing. "Applause" could be any sound members of an audience make when they like what they're seeing.

Encourage both the actors and the rest of the group members to "ham it up" in their assigned roles.

Afterward, point out: **The sweet young girl in this skit went through several different emotions. What were some of them?** (Sadness, fear, relief, happiness.)

Have you ever had a day in which you experienced several different emotions in a short period of time? Encourage several group members to share their experiences. If you think they'd be comfortable talking about it, ask them to explain what events and circumstances influenced their emotions that day. You may want to be prepared to share an example from your own life to "break the ice."

STEP
2

Circumstances

Ask: **What usually causes your emotions to change? For instance, if you're feeling sad, what might cause you to feel happy?** Help group members recognize that events and circumstances play a large role in determining our emotions.

Explain: **I'm going to read a list of different situations. After I read each one, let me know what emotions you would probably feel in that situation and how strongly you would feel them.** Group members will indicate their emotions by calling them out to you. They will indicate how strongly they would feel those emotions by the volume of their voices. Whispers will indicate that their emotions wouldn't be very strong. Shouts will indicate that their emotions would be overpowering.

The situations are as follows:

(1) Your teacher is passing out a test that you haven't studied for at all. (Possible responses: Nervousness, fear, regret, etc.)

(2) Your teacher is passing out a test that you've studied hard for all week. (Possible responses: Confidence, happiness, excitement, etc.)

(3) You're sitting in a dentist's chair, and your dentist is getting ready to drill a hole in your tooth. (Possible responses: Nervousness, fear, panic, etc.)

(4) You've just been caught in a lie by your parents. (Possible responses: Nervousness, fear, regret, etc.)

(5) You just found out that the person at school you have a crush on tried to call you last night while you were out with your family. (Possible responses: Excitement, nervousness, regret, etc.)

(6) Your best friend just moved to another state to live. (Possible responses: Sadness, fear, regret, etc.)

Afterward, ask: **Are emotions good or bad?** Get responses from as many group members as possible.

Then say: **That's like asking whether arms and legs are bad, or hair and hands. Emotions are just part of us. We were created with them.**

OPTIONS

SMALL GROUP

FELLOWSHIP & WORSHIP

MOSTLY GIRLS

MOSTLY GUYS

EXTRA FUN

SHORT MEETING TIME

URBAN

JR. HIGH HIGH SCHOOL COMBINED

SIXTH GRADE

In Whose Image?

(Needed: Bibles)

Have group members turn in their Bibles to Genesis 1:27. Read the verse aloud together as a group.

Then ask: **Who created the man and woman?** (God.)

According to this verse, how were the man and woman created? (In God's image.)

If we're created in God's image, and we have emotions, does that mean God has emotions too? If so, which emotions do you think God experiences? Encourage several group members to offer their opinions.

Have someone read aloud John 3:16. Then ask: **What emotion is God identified with in this verse?** (Love.)

Is this the same kind of love we feel for others? (Human love is often conditional. We love people who love us or who do nice things for us. When we speak of God's love, we're really talking about more than a feeling. It is the attitude or will that seeks the best for us. God's love is a perfect, unconditional love. It's not based on anything we do for Him. Romans 5:8 tells us that even when we were sinners, God loved us enough to send His Son to die for us.)

Have someone read aloud Numbers 32:13. Then ask: **What emotion is God identified with in this passage?** (Anger.)

Is this the same kind of anger we feel for others? (Human anger is usually based on revenge. When someone does something to us, we get angry and usually desire to "get back" at the person. Because God is holy and perfect, His anger is directed at sin. His anger is not based on revenge or other insecure human emotions.)

Have someone read aloud Exodus 20:5. Then ask: **What emotion is God identified with in this passage?** (Jealousy.)

Is this the same kind of jealousy we experience? (Human jealousy is based on insecurity. When people get jealous, it's usually because their fragile egos have been wounded. It's tough to accept that people prefer others to us. God's jealousy is based on His perfection. God created us; God is perfect; and God is the one, true God. For these reasons, He alone deserves our worship. When we put other "gods" in His place—after all He's done for us—we are denying His rightful authority and position. Therefore, His jealousy is justified.)

Point out that if God's emotions are perfect and ours are imperfect,

God might be a good source to turn to when we have questions about or problems with our emotions.

A Time for Everything

(Needed: Bible, paper, pencils)

Distribute a piece of paper and a pencil to each group member. Then give the following instructions: **Tear this sheet of paper into four sections. On one section, write down an everyday situation or event that could cause you to get *angry*. On another section, write down an everyday situation or event that could make you *happy*. On another section, write down an everyday situation or event that could make you *sad*. On the final section, write down an everyday situation or event that could make you feel *scared*.**

After group members have written their responses, have them label the back of each section ("angry," "happy," "sad," and "scared"). Collect the slips of paper, keeping each emotion category separate.

Have group members form four teams. Assign each team one of the emotion categories, and give that team three slips of paper from the corresponding stack. If possible, look through the slips before you distribute them. Make sure you don't distribute any slips that are too personal or that would identify the people who wrote them.

Instruct the members of the "angry," "sad," and "scared" teams to read their situations and then come up with ideas for how God could help someone facing those situations. For instance, let's say the "scared" team is assigned the following situation: "Every day I'm afraid that I won't have anyone to sit with at lunch." Team members may suggest that God could help someone facing this situation by bringing a group of friends into this person's life or by giving the person the courage to sit with people he or she doesn't know.

Instruct the members of the "happy" team to read their situations and then come up with ideas for how God could be honored and praised in those situations. For instance, let's say the team is assigned the following situation: "Buying new clothes makes me happy." Team members may suggest that God could be honored if the person would take a certain percentage of his or her clothes money and give it to the church or to the needy.

O P T I O N S

EXTRA ACTION

LARGE GROUP

HEARD IT ALL BEFORE

LITTLE BIBLE BACKGROUND

FELLOWSHIP & WORSHIP

MOSTLY GIRLS

SIXTH GRADE

Give the teams a few minutes to work. When they're finished, have each team share its situations and responses with the rest of the group.

Afterward, say: **Think about the ideas we've just heard for including God in our emotional lives. Choose one idea that sounded good to you. Make a commitment to use that idea the next time you get angry, happy, sad, or scared.** Give group members a minute or two to consider the ideas. If you have time, ask a couple of volunteers to share the ideas they chose.

As you wrap up the session, have someone read aloud Ecclesiastes 3:1-8. Ask group members to call out other suggestions for this passage—perhaps suggestions that are relevant to their everyday experiences.

For instance, group members might suggest that there is
• a time for studying and a time for goofing off;
• a time for being excited and a time for being reserved;
• a time for getting angry and a time for patching things up;
• a time to feel scared and a time to feel confident.

Emphasize that there is a time for every emotion and a time to ask for God's help with those emotions.

Close the session in prayer, thanking God that He created us with the ability to experience a wide range of emotions and that He's always available to help us with our emotions.

A TRIP TO
GRANDMOTHER'S HOUSE

NARRATOR: One day, many years ago, a sweet young girl (**CUTE SOUND**) was sitting at the breakfast table talking with her kind and caring mother (**CUTE SOUND**).

MOTHER: Oh, my sweet young daughter (**CUTE SOUND**), I have terrible news for you. Your grandmother is feeling ill (**CRYING SOUND**). She needs you to take her some soup (**YUMMY SOUND**).

YOUNG GIRL: What kind of soup (**YUMMY SOUND**) shall I take her?

MOTHER: Her favorite—cream of mustard (**YUMMY SOUND**).

NARRATOR: Before the sweet young girl (**CUTE SOUND**) left the house with the hot, homemade cream of mustard soup (**YUMMY SOUND**), her mother said…

MOTHER: Be careful on your way to Grandmother's house. Do not talk to any mean and terrible strangers (**BOO, HISS**). You know that mean and terrible strangers (**BOO, HISS**) love soup (**YUMMY SOUND**). They may hurt you (**CRYING SOUND**) if you refuse to give it to them.

NARRATOR: With this warning, the sweet young girl (**CUTE SOUND**) left. On the way to her grandmother's house, who should appear before her but a mean and terrible stranger (**BOO, HISS**)!

STRANGER: Give me that hot, homemade soup (**YUMMY SOUND**) or I'll bite your nose off!

YOUNG GIRL: No, no, I must not—for if I do, my grandmother will have nothing to eat (**CRYING SOUND**). And she so loves her cream of mustard soup. (**YUMMY SOUND**)

STRANGER: Cream of *mustard* soup (**YUMMY SOUND**)?

NARRATOR: Just then, a strong and noble young man (**APPLAUSE**) came along.

YOUNG MAN: Away with you, you mean and terrible stranger (**BOO, HISS**).

NARRATOR: The mean and terrible stranger (**BOO, HISS**) ran away, fearing for his life. As he ran, he yelled back over his shoulder…

STRANGER: I don't even like cream of mustard soup (**YUMMY SOUND**)! Why don't you teach your mother to make something normal, like chicken noodle soup (**BOO, HISS**) or beef stew (**BOO, HISS**)?

NARRATOR: The moral of this story is "Never talk to mean and terrible strangers (**BOO, HISS**)—especially when you're a sweet young girl (**CUTE SOUND**) carrying hot, homemade cream of mustard soup (**YUMMY SOUND**) to your grandmother (**APPLAUSE**)!

Step 1

Have a sound-effects contest along with the skit. Before the actors begin, have the rest of the students form Teams A and B. Give them time to look over the skit and figure out how to make each sound effect unique every time it is used during the skit. For example, unique ways to say the cute "ahhh" sound would be for a team to whisper it or to sing it in harmony. Have teams take turns going first.

Step 4

Write the following emotions on index cards: happy, angry, excited, confident, sad, scared, nervous, jealous, and vengeful. Have group members form teams. Give one index card to each team along with a stack of newspapers, old magazines, and tape. Have each team use the supplies to creatively "dress" one of its members to look like the emotion that is written on the team's index card. For example, to make a person look angry or vengeful, kids could wrap their teammate like a mummy and tape long horns made out of crushed, rolled-up newspaper to his or her head. Have each team's "dressed up" member stand, walk around, or act while each team member describes an everyday situation or event that could cause him or her to feel the emotion printed on the card. If the emotion is negative, have kids come up with ideas for how God could help them in those negative situations; if the emotion is positive, have them come up with ways to honor or praise God in those situations.

Step 1

Skip the skit. Instead, have kids "chart" their emotions for a day or a week. Distribute pencils and paper. Have kids draw two intersecting lines near the lower left corner of their papers. Along the vertical line, they should write numbers one through five, with one at the bottom (representing not much emotion) and five at the top (representing hit-the-ceiling emotion). Along the horizontal line, they should write key words or draw symbols to represent people or events that elicited an emotion last week (in the order in which the events happened). Some graphs may resemble wild roller coaster rides; others may resemble gently rolling hills. Ask volunteers to explain their charts. Then have them make separate charts that represent what they wish their emotional charts would look like. Ask: **How is your made-up chart different from your real one? What things tend to cause you to feel really emotional? What kinds of things don't bother you much?**

Step 2

A small group of kids may feel put on the spot by all of the questions in this step. So cut down on the number of situations you describe that ask kids to identify their emotional responses. Just read a few of the six situations. Choose a mixture of negative and positive ones. Or simply read some of the emotions and have kids supply events in life that might lead to those particular emotions.

Step 3

Involve more kids by creating small groups and having them look up more Scripture passages about God's emotions. Have them answer these questions for each passage: **What emotion is God identified with in this passage? Is this the same kind of emotion we experience? Why or why not?** Suggested passages include John 2:13-17 (anger, enthusiasm); Romans 15:13 (hope); Zephaniah 1:18; Exodus 34:14; Deuteronomy 6:15 (jealousy); Jeremiah 33:9 (joy); Proverbs 6:16-19 (hate); Matthew 18:12-14 (happiness); Nahum 1:2 (vengeance); Hebrews 1:9 (hate, joy); Exodus 20:6; Matthew 3:16, 17 (love).

Step 4

A creative way to help a large group relate more to the closing prayer is to have someone bring in a baby just before you pray. Have kids watch the baby for a few minutes while it plays, interacts with its mother or father, or cries about something it needs or wants. After the baby leaves, have everyone settle down. The baby will have reminded your kids in a fresh way of the range of emotions that God gave us, which might help them to better tune in to the prayer.

Step 3

What do you do with kids who think, "Emotions? Made in God's image? So what! Image schmimage!"? You get kids with this attitude to create a skit in which earthlings try to describe various emotions to an emotionless alien like Spock from *Star Trek*. To get them started, you could tell them to build a skit around a description of rage, like this: **Rage feels like a river of pain pulsing through your body after you step on ten sharp nails that pierce deep into your foot. The river of rage races up your legs, into your chest, through your neck, and explodes out of your head like a nuclear blast. Hate and anger spurt from your mouth and fingernails, forever staining, even maiming, anyone or anything near you.** Have kids take turns trying to describe emotions, like fear, love, joy, surprise, sorrow, pity, etc. Discuss Scripture passages that talk about how our emotions have been warped by sin (Romans 1:28-32) and how God can help us deal with overwhelming emotions (Psalm 71:20, 21; Romans 8:18-27).

Step 4

Don't let the closing prayer go by unnoticed at the end of this step. Make it a special time by suddenly changing the pace of the session. Encourage kids to stop rustling papers, shifting in their seats, or whispering. Remind them that they are about to approach God's throne. You may even want to pray in hushed tones to bring attention to the fact that something very important is going on. You might turn off the bright lights and light a candle or bring a small lamp that sheds a soft light.

Step 3

To give your kids a little more background about what it means to be created in the image of God, read aloud this updated version of a passage from Martin Luther's *Commentary on Genesis*. Point out that much of it is speculation on Luther's part. **When God created Adam, He created a beautiful, excellent, noble creature. Adam wasn't sick from sin. All of his senses were perfect and pure. His mind was clear, his memory was complete, his will was sincere. He didn't fear death and didn't worry about anything. Adam was strong and beautiful physically. He was greater than any other creature God made. I believe that before Adam sinned, his eyesight was so good that his vision was more powerful than that of the lynx. I believe that Adam was so strong that he could handle full-grown lions and bears as if they were cubs. I also believe that food tasted better to Adam before he sinned.** Ask kids if they agree or disagree and why.

Step 4

By now your kids will have learned that God has emotions. But some of your kids may not know much else about God. So they might not feel comfortable when you encourage them to turn to a stranger (God) for help when they feel emotionally distraught. If you suspect that some of your kids feel this way, you may want to take time to talk about who God is and what He has done for us. You can refer to the classic *Knowing God* by J. I. Packer (InterVarsity Press), which examines the nature and character of God. Draw a few key concepts from it. Or, to explain the Gospel clearly and succinctly, read and discuss the following verses: Jeremiah 31:3; Romans 3:23; 6:23; John 3:16, 17; Romans 10:9; 1 Corinthians 15:3, 4; 1 John 5:11; John 10:10.

Step 2

In large print, write down colors and associated emotions on separate sheets of paper. (For example: red/angry, blue/sad, black/depressed, yellow/happy, etc.) Post the sheets around the room. If possible, assign kids to groups based on a color they are wearing. Randomly shift kids around if some groups are larger than others. Give someone in each group a pencil and paper to record the group's response to this question: **What kinds of things have caused you to experience the emotion you have been assigned?** Also have group members come up with Scripture verses that describe people (or God) experiencing a similar emotion. Each group should present its personal stories and Bible stories to the other groups.

Step 4

At the end of your session, give kids a chance to relax and eat together while continuing to teach them something about emotions. Set a table for them to eat at. Then tell them that you are going to provide them with a wonderful snack. Bring out a bowl of brussels sprouts, lemon wedges, or lima beans. After the protests die down, bring out the real snack—something kids will like. In a low-key way, you can talk about the difference between feeling disappointed or angry and satisfied or happy. Encourage kids to tell God about their disappointments *and* their joys.

Step 2

As you talk about whether group members think of emotions as being either "good" or "bad," ask if they know why they answered as they did. Say: **Since emotions are just a normal part of us, does this mean we can use our emotions in either a "good" way or a "bad" way? Can you think of an example of someone using a normal emotion in an appropriate way? In an inappropriate way? Is it possible for girls to use emotions as an excuse to justify wrong behavior? If so, give some examples.**

Step 4

After the members of the teams have been given their situations, ask them to plan a skit to demonstrate at least one positive way someone could handle that situation and one negative way to handle it. If possible, provide some materials for props. After a few minutes, have the teams present their skits.

Step 1

If you have mostly guys in your group, you may need to loosen them up a bit so that they are more willing to talk about emotions. The skit may help you do that because it is lighthearted enough to be nonthreatening. Guys may also like it if you create a more competitive atmosphere by having auditions for the skit parts and for the privilege of making the sound effects. The more creative and expressive they are, the more likely they will be awarded a part or sound effect.

Step 2

Some guys may feel uncomfortable answering the first question because it is personal. You might want to generalize the question in this way: **What usually causes someone's emotions to change? For instance, if someone is feeling sad, what might cause him or her to feel happy?** Here are some other situations you might want to use:
• **Your favorite baseball team just choked and lost the final play-off game.**
• **A bunch of guys are teasing you about your voice changing.**
• **It's a beautiful day outside and the church service looks like it's never going to end.**
• **It's really stormy outside and the sirens go off because a tornado (or hurricane) is moving your way.**

Step 1

Add a fun twist to the skit by assigning the male roles to girls and the female roles to guys. Guys should try to talk in a higher voice while the girls talk in lower voices. The guy who plays the sweet young girl could pretend he has long hair that he twists around his finger when he talks. The girl who plays the stranger could talk with a tough accent and flex her muscles. Add a crazy twist to the narrator's part by having two narrators take turns reading every other word. Or add to the fun with props like a picnic basket or soup tureen, wigs, skirts for the guys, a trench coat, fake mustaches, etc.

Step 2

Create an atmosphere in which kids feel all kinds of emotions. Pump kids up by promising unusual or outrageous prizes (if you dare), then playing a few high-energy, very competitive, challenging relays. You could promise the winning team a concert or sports outing. Or before the games begin, you could have all players sign contracts promising to personally serve the winners for a day or a week. Losers could promise to make the winners' beds, do their laundry, make meals or treats, etc. If personal weekday contact is impossible, kids could sign contracts to make a complete dinner for the winners at your next session. After the games, talk about the different emotions kids may have felt as they played (excitement, disappointment, anxiety, etc.).

Step 1
During the week, videotape a dozen or so brief segments from TV shows or movies that show people expressing various emotions (being careful to avoid sexually explicit or gory scenes, of course). When you play the tape, have kids identify each emotion and give a thumbs-up signal if it is a healthy way to express emotion or a thumbs-down signal if it is unhealthy. Then ask: **Have you ever had a day in which you experienced several different emotions in a short period of time?**

Step 3
Play a current secular love song about disappointment, miscommunication, conditional love, or regret. You can use the song to compare and contrast the world's concept of love with God's love as expressed in John 3:16. Or clip a review of a popular movie that represents unhealthy ways in which people deal with anger. (A good example is a scene from *Batman Returns*. In revenge, Catwoman gives her boss a deadly kiss.) Compare and contrast God's anger with human anger.

Step 1
Combine Steps 1 and 2. Read the following scenario: **A company has just invented a button that changes color to show whatever emotion you are feeling at the time—red means you're angry, blue means your depressed, green means you're jealous, and so on. Your school just bought a bunch of the buttons and kids are required to wear them whenever they're on the school grounds.** Have group members form teams to answer these questions:
• **What would be the positive things about the emotion buttons?**
• **What would be the negative things about the emotion buttons?**
• **When would/wouldn't you want to wear the buttons?**
• **What colors would your button have been during your most recent school day?**

   As you discuss the circumstances in Step 2, continue to refer to the buttons and their changing colors.

Step 2
If you don't even have time for the button exercise described above, skip Step 1 entirely. Have kids stand up. Explain to them that they're going to get some exercise. It's a new concept called "Facial Aerobics." Every time you call out an emotion (or a circumstance), kids are to demonstrate that particular emotion with a facial expression or some other body movement. Here are some emotions you might use: fear, disgust, joy, surprise, anger, and sadness. You might also use these situations:
• **You're about to take a test you haven't studied for.**
• **You wake up and find out that school's been canceled.**
• **Your best friend just told you he or she is moving to another state.**
• **Your favorite team just won the championship.**

Step 2
For an urban group, you might want to use the following situations:
(1) The car you borrowed has just been stolen.
(2) A home pregnancy test has shown that you (or your girlfriend) are positively pregnant.
(3) The doctor orders you to stay home for ten days because you have chicken pox. Now you can't go to the amusement park tomorrow.
(4) You just received $5,000 for turning in a wanted fugitive.
(5) The fugitive you turned in just escaped from prison.
(6) You broke a window while playing stickball.
(7) You get punched in the eye and mouth while trying to break up a fight.

Step 3
After answering the questions associated with Numbers 32:13, mention that our anger and God's anger are often pointed in two different directions. Ours tends to involve revenge, while God's involves renewal. We take sin against us personally and try to harm. God seeks to reconcile the sinner to not do it again. Read the following anger scenarios and have teens decide how they could respond with reconciliation, not vengeance.
• **You are ticked off because someone just cursed at your mother and said degrading things about her. You're steaming. How do you respond?**
• **The $80 watch you just bought is missing. You saw it last in your locker, but overheard who stole it. How do you respond?**

Step 1
Be sensitive to junior high kids who might feel uncomfortable acting in the skit in front of high schoolers. You could help them feel more comfortable by offering junior highers small roles (such as the mother or the noble young man) or roles that don't require any acting (such as the narrator). Or you could have junior highers serve as some of the props. For example, a high schooler could play the sweet young girl and could carry a junior higher who has the word "soup" pinned to his or her shirt. If high schoolers think the skit is beneath them, have them create skits of their own in which a person experiences as many emotions as possible in a very short time. Suggest one or more of the following scenarios: the first day of school; a kid applying to a college; a spectator at a football game; a driving instructor.

Step 2
Give kids the opportunity to interact with someone their own age by pairing up high schoolers with high schoolers and junior highers with junior highers. Then have the partners tell each other their answer to this question: **What usually causes your emotions to change? For instance, if you're feeling sad, what might cause you to feel happy?** Tell them to come up with responses that weren't discussed earlier.

Step 2
As you discuss the different situations, make a list on the board of the emotions named. Ask your sixth graders to describe and define the words and talk about their experiences with these emotions. Ask: **Have you experienced most or all of these emotions? How about in the last twenty-four hours? Can you choose which emotions you will experience? Why or why not?**

Step 4
Instead of asking all of your sixth graders to write about four different emotions, have them tear their papers into two sections and write about two emotions. Ask one half of the group to write about an event that could cause them to be angry and about something that would make them happy. Have the others write about events that would make them sad and events that would make them scared. Collect the papers, keeping each emotion category separate, and continue the activity as described.

Date Used: _____

Approx.
Time

Step 1: Emotions on Display _____
o Extra Action
o Small Group
o Mostly Guys
o Extra Fun
o Media
o Short Meeting Time
o Combined Junior High/High School
Things needed:

Step 2: Circumstances _____
o Small Group
o Fellowship & Worship
o Mostly Girls
o Mostly Guys
o Extra Fun
o Short Meeting Time
o Urban
o Combined Junior High/High School
o Sixth Grade
Things needed:

Step 3: In Whose Image? _____
o Large Group
o Heard It All Before
o Little Bible Background
o Media
o Urban
Things needed:

Step 4: A Time for Everything _____
o Extra Action
o Large Group
o Heard It All Before
o Little Bible Background
o Fellowship & Worship
o Mostly Girls
o Sixth Grade
Things needed:

2 Sad, Glad, and Back Again

YOUR GOALS FOR THIS SESSION:

Choose one or more

☐ To help kids recognize which situations cause them to feel certain emotions.

☐ To help kids understand how God can help us with any emotion we experience.

☐ To help kids choose a promise from God's Word that will help them understand His role in their emotions.

☐ Other _____

_____

Your Bible Base:

Psalm 31

A Lot of Hot Air

(Needed: Balloons, markers, chalkboard and chalk or newsprint and marker [optional])

Ask: **How many different emotions would you say you experience in an average day?** Encourage group members to name the different emotions they might experience. You may want to list the emotions on the board as they are named. Among the emotions that might be named are happiness, sadness, anger, disappointment, fear, anxiety, jealousy, revenge, hatred, etc.

Do you think it's normal to go through so many different emotions in one day? (Yes. Our emotions are usually our reaction to events and circumstances in our lives. As those events and circumstances change, our emotions usually change.)

Say: **Let's take a closer look at four of the most common emotions we face.**

Have group members form four teams. Distribute a balloon and several markers to each team. Assign each team one of the following emotions: happiness, sadness, anger, and disappointment. Instruct the teams to come up with a brief scenario, using the balloons, to illustrate their assigned emotions.

For instance, members of the "anger" team might inflate their balloon (without tying it), draw a scowling face on it, and then deflate it. Then they could brainstorm several different events and circumstances that could make a person angry.

When they make their presentation, they could hold up their balloon and say, "This is Bob Balloon. He's not having a very good day today. This morning his little brother ate all the Cap'n Crunch, so the only cereal left for Bob was Bran Flakes." Then someone could blow up the balloon a little to indicate Bob's anger. "On the way to school, Bob was walking too close to a mud puddle in the street when a car went by. Bob was soaked from the waist down. He didn't have time to go home and change, so he had to wear the wet clothes to school." Then someone could blow up the balloon a little more to indicate Bob's growing anger. The team could continue blowing up the balloon little by little, until it explodes.

Give the teams several minutes to work. When everyone is finished, have each team make its presentation. Lead the group in a round of applause after each presentation.

Collect the balloons after the presentations have been made, so they don't become a distraction later in the session.

Say What You Feel

(Needed: Two sheets of newsprint or poster board, markers, masking tape)

Have group members form two teams. Give each team a sheet of newsprint or poster board and several markers. Instruct the members of one team to create a sign with the following words on it: "Happy," "Wonderful, "Great," and "Awesome." They should use bright colors and cheerful designs (smiling faces, sunshine, etc.) for the sign.

Instruct the members of the other team to create a sign with the following words on it: "Terrible," "Rotten," "Difficult," and "The Worst." They should use dark colors and depressing designs (frowning faces, storm clouds, etc.) for the sign.

When the teams are finished, have them tape the signs on opposite sides of the room. Then have everyone gather in the middle of the room.

Explain: **I'm going to read a list of questions. After I read each one, I want you to go to the side of the room that best answers that question.**

For instance, I might ask, "How was your last trip to the dentist?" If your last visit to the dentist's office was happy, wonderful, great, or awesome, you would stand on that side of the room. Point to the appropriate side of the room. **If the visit was terrible, rotten, difficult, or the worst, you would stand on that side of the room.** Point to the other side of the room. **If the visit was kind of good, kind of bad, or just so-so, you'd stand somewhere in the middle of the room to show that.**

Use as many of the following questions as are appropriate for your group. You may even want to come up with some questions of your own.

- **How was your day at school today** (or **Friday**)?
- **How was your lunch today?**
- **How did you do on the last test you took at school?**
- **How was the last conversation you had with one of your parents?**

• **How is your relationship with the guy or girl you're interested in?**
• **How is your relationship with your best friend?**
• **How is your relationship with your brothers and sisters?**
• **How do you feel about life in general?**

Afterward, ask: **How much of an influence do circumstances and events have on a person's emotions?** (Circumstances and events have a *direct* impact on a person's emotions. If things are going well for the person, he or she is usually happy. If things aren't going well, his or her emotions usually will reflect it.)

STEP 3

Emotional Rescue

(Needed: Copies of Repro Resource 2, colored pens or markers)

Ask: **If circumstances and events have such a big influence on us, does that mean we're helpless to control our emotions? For instance, when we're sad, do we have to wait for something good to happen before we can get happy again?** Get responses from as many group members as possible.

Where can we find help for our emotions? (From God, from the Bible.)

Hold up a Bible. Ask: **Have you ever thought of this as an "emotional" book?** Get a few responses.

Point out that probably every emotion we will ever experience is addressed in the Bible—whether it's practical advice for dealing with a specific emotion ("Do not let the sun go down while you are still angry" [Ephesians 4:26]) or stories about how certain Bible characters handled their emotions.

Explain: **Probably one of the most emotional books of the Bible is the Book of Psalms. Most of the Psalms were written by David, a man who was very close to God. As part of his closeness with God, David often shared his innermost emotions and feelings in his writings. From these writings, we can get an idea of how God feels about our emotions.**

Have group members form pairs. Distribute copies of "Emotions in Motion" (Repro Resource 2) and several colored pens or markers to each pair.

Instruct the pairs to read through the sheet (which is the text of

OPTIONS

EXTRA ACTION

LARGE GROUP

HEARD IT ALL BEFORE

LITTLE BIBLE BACKGROUND

FELLOWSHIP & WORSHIP

MOSTLY GIRLS

SIXTH GRADE

Psalm 31) and circle any words that have to do with emotions. Instruct the pairs to use different colors to indicate different kinds of emotions. For instance, they might use yellow to indicate happy or joyful emotions; they might use blue to indicate depressed or sad emotions; they might use green to indicate jealous or envious emotions; they might use purple to indicate hateful emotions; they might use red to indicate angry emotions; etc.

Give the pairs several minutes to work. When they're finished, go through Repro Resource 2 as a group. Have volunteers take turns reading Psalm 31 aloud. As a volunteer reads each verse, the other group members will call out any emotion words they circled in that verse, and explain what color they used and why.

Among the words that might be circled are "shame" (vs. 1), "hate" (vs. 6), "glad and rejoice" (vs. 7), "anguish" (vs. 7), "distress" (vs. 9), "sorrow" (vs. 9), "grief" (vs. 9), "anguish" (vs. 10), and "shame" (vs. 17). In addition, verses 11-13 seem to address emotions like worthlessness and fear.

Why do you think David shared his emotions with God? (Perhaps it made him feel better to know that God knew what he was feeling. Perhaps he wanted God's help in dealing with his emotions.)

What phrases in Psalm 31 describe the kind of comfort David was looking for from God during David's time of emotional distress? ("In you, O Lord, I have taken refuge," "let me never be put to shame," "deliver me in your righteousness" [vs. 1]; "turn your ear to me," "come quickly to my rescue" [vs. 2]; "lead and guide me" [vs. 3]; "Be merciful to me, O Lord, for I am in distress" [vs. 9]; "let me not be put to shame" [vs. 17].)

Do you think God answered David's requests? (By the number of praises in David's psalms and the thankful tone of his writing, it's probably safe to say that God answered David's requests.)

If you were feeling angry or sad or even happy, do you think sharing your emotions with God would help you feel any better? Explain your answer. Encourage group members to respond honestly.

STEP

4

Help from a Friend

(Needed: Different-colored balloons, strings, slips of paper, pencils, tape, copies of Repro Resource 2)

Say: **Just like David, we can find comfort and help from God when our emotions get the better of us. In fact, we can probably find that comfort and help in David's writings.**

Set out several different-colored balloons, pieces of string, slips of paper, and pencils. Instruct each group member to choose a balloon whose color represents an emotion he or she would like to take to God. For instance, if someone wanted God's help for sadness or depression, he or she might choose a blue balloon; if someone wanted God's help for anger, he or she might choose a red balloon; etc.

After a group member has chosen a balloon, he or she should blow it up and tie a piece of string to it. Then he or she should look through Repro Resource 2 and find a verse or statement that could provide comfort or help for dealing with his or her chosen emotion. (For instance, verse 9 might be a good prayer for someone who is sad or depressed. Verse 22 might be a helpful reminder for someone who is scared or lonely. And verse 7 could be a source of comfort for practically any troubling emotion.)

Have each group member write his or her verse on a slip of paper and then tape the paper to the balloon string.

Encourage group members to take their balloons home as reminders of God's willingness to help us with our emotions. Then, whenever they feel overwhelmed by their emotions, they can look at the verse they wrote down for comfort.

Close the session in prayer, thanking God for comforting us and helping us with our emotions.

O P T I O N S

EXTRA ACTION

HEARD IT ALL BEFORE

LITTLE BIBLE BACKGROUND

FELLOWSHIP & WORSHIP

MOSTLY GIRLS

MOSTLY GUYS

EXTRA FUN

MEDIA

SHORT MEETING TIME

URBAN

SIXTH GRADE

EMOTIONS IN MOTION

PSALM 31

1 In you, O Lord, I have taken refuge; let me never be put to shame; deliver me in your righteousness.

2 Turn your ear to me, come quickly to my rescue; be my rock of refuge, a strong fortress to save me.

3 Since you are my rock and my fortress, for the sake of your name lead and guide me.

4 Free me from the trap that is set for me, for you are my refuge.

5 Into your hands I commit my spirit; redeem me, O Lord, the God of truth.

6 I hate those who cling to worthless idols; I trust in the Lord.

7 I will be glad and rejoice in your love, for you saw my affliction and knew the anguish of my soul.

8 You have not handed me over to the enemy but have set my feet in a spacious place.

9 Be merciful to me, O Lord, for I am in distress; my eyes grow weak with sorrow, my soul and my body with grief.

10 My life is consumed by anguish and my years by groaning; my strength fails because of my affliction, and my bones grow weak.

11 Because of all my enemies, I am the utter contempt of my neighbors; I am a dread to my friends—those who see me on the street flee from me.

12 I am forgotten by them as though I were dead; I have become like broken pottery.

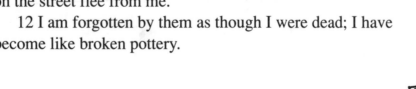

2b

13 For I hear the slander of many; there is terror on every side; they conspire against me and plot to take my life.

14 But I trust in you, O Lord; I say, "You are my God."

15 My times are in your hands; deliver me from my enemies and from those who pursue me.

16 Let your face shine on your servant; save me in your unfailing love.

17 Let me not be put to shame, O Lord, for I have cried out to you; but let the wicked be put to shame and lie silent in the grave.

18 Let their lying lips be silenced, for with pride and contempt they speak arrogantly against the righteous.

19 How great is your goodness, which you have stored up for those who fear you, which you bestow in the sight of men on those who take refuge in you.

20 In the shelter of your presence you hide them from the intrigues of men; in your dwelling you keep them safe from accusing tongues.

21 Praise be to the Lord, for he showed his wonderful love to me when I was in a besieged city.

22 In my alarm I said, "I am cut off from your sight!" Yet you heard my cry for mercy when I called to you for help.

23 Love the Lord, all his saints! The Lord preserves the faithful, but the proud he pays back in full.

24 Be strong and take heart, all you who hope in the Lord.

Step 3

Instead of having pairs of kids circle emotional words on "Emotions in Motion" (Repro Resource 2), have teams of three or more kids do something a little different with it. Assign each team three to five verses from the sheet. Have the members of each team present their verses by standing up and linking arms. As a volunteer from the team reads the verses aloud, the rest of the team should demonstrate each emotion with their faces or with gestures (arms still linked). They should say the word aloud and softly until another emotional word is read. For example, team members assigned the first group of verses might hang their heads and softly say, "Shame, shame, shame . . ."

Step 4

Distribute a balloon, a long piece of string, a slip of paper, and a pencil to each group member. Instruct each group member to write an emotion on his or her slip of paper and then insert the slip into the deflated balloon. Then have each kid blow up his or her balloon, tie one end of the string to the balloon, and tie the other end of the string to his or her ankle. Have a contest in which kids try to pop each other's balloons by stepping on them. If a person pops someone else's balloon, he or she collects the slip of paper that was inside. The object of the game is for group members to get as many different emotions as possible. Afterward, briefly discuss the various emotions that were written on the slips. Then go through Step 4 as written.

Step 1

Depending on how small your group is, you might want to have kids work in pairs instead of teams to come up with the balloon scenarios. Or you might have only two teams each address an emotion. If you use only two teams, make sure you assign one of them "happiness," so that there's a balance between a positive emotion and a negative one.

Step 2

Instead of having two teams create colorful signs that might take a lot of teamwork and artwork, give each group member three index cards. On one card, group members should write "happy," "wonderful," "great," or "awesome." On the second card, they should write "so-so" or "OK." On the third card, they should write "terrible," "rotten," "difficult," or "the worst." Then, instead of having kids move from one side of the room to the other in response to the questions you ask, they can hold up their individual cards to show how they feel.

Step 1

Set up two "emotion stations" in the room. You'll need a table, a chair, several rolls of tape, and a box at each station. Fill one box with slips of paper on which you've written instructions (one per slip) that will make kids happy. (For example: "Get a dollar from your leader." "Get a free soda on our next outing." "Get two compliments from your leader.") Fill the box at the other station with instructions that will irritate kids. (For example: "Give a quarter to your leader." "Keep your hands on your knees for the next five minutes.") Ask for one or two volunteers to work at each station. Divide the other kids into two teams; assign each team to one of the stations. Instruct kids to draw a slip from the box, read it, tape it to their shirts, and do what it says (if applicable). The station leader should initial the papers as kids follow through on them. Afterward, talk about how happy or irritated groups members felt about their instruction. Then introduce the topic of emotions.

Step 3

Get kids to open up about the emotions they feel by creating teams. Give a bowl filled with nuts or small candies to each team. Say: **David felt a lot of different emotions, and so do we. But we don't always get to talk about our feelings. Take as many pieces of candy as you want. But you will have to talk about one emotion you felt this week for every piece you take.**

Step 3

Kids who have spent a lot of time in church may have heard plenty of statements like these: "God knows how you feel." "He can help you when you are upset." "A lot of people in the Bible expressed their emotions to God." Grab the attention of your skeptics and make this session even more relevant to them by challenging them with this simulation: **The year is 2141. You have just been appointed the leader of a country that is in terrible trouble. No one in this country has talked about his or her emotions for decades. No one has said "I'm angry," "I'm sad," or "I'm happy" for thirty years. Some people are starting to feel as if they are going to explode because they have bottled up their feelings for so long; others are too depressed to even think about exploding. As the new leader, you are called upon to solve this problem. What do you do and why?**

Step 4

Jaded kids may not have thought seriously about why it's important to seek God's help in dealing with their emotions. Present two extreme ways of mishandling emotions and have kids list their consequences. The first extreme is keeping emotions bottled up. Instead of asking kids how to solve this problem, have them identify and discuss the consequences of living this way. The second extreme is expressing emotions without restraint. What if everyone who was angry screamed all of the time at the top of his or her lungs? What if everyone who was happy was sickeningly joyful for brief periods? What if people felt so much hate that there was no room for any other emotion? Some of the consequences of out-of-control emotions are exhaustion, depression, or even violence. Discuss what life would be like if all people were overly emotional. Then talk about how to strike the right balance.

Step 3

Give a little more background on David. Help kids understand that he experienced all kinds of wonderful and terrible things throughout his life that resulted in feelings of great joy, sorrow, fear, and worry. Read or briefly describe highlights of his life, such as these: I Samuel 16:1, 13 (David is anointed king); I Samuel 18:6-11 (Saul tries to murder David); 20:16, 41, 42 (Jonathan and David's friendship); 27:1 (David is afraid of being murdered); II Samuel 1:11, 12 (David mourns Jonathan); 7:8, 9 (God promises David great things); 11:1-5 and 12:15-22 (David commits adultery); 19:1-4 (David mourns Absalom).

Step 4

Some kids may not understand how God's Word—particularly the Psalms—can be a source of comfort and help to them. Reassure them that these ancient thoughts and feelings do apply to their lives today. Have them highlight the following phrases from "Emotions in Motion" (Repro Resource 2). Rephrase each statement in contemporary terms in the form of a question. For example, have kids highlight "put to shame." Then ask: **Have you ever seen someone humiliated? What happened? What does it feel like to be humiliated?** You can have kids highlight these phrases or others that you think apply to their lives: "free me from the trap that is set for me" (Psalm 31:4); "I will be glad and rejoice in your love" (vs. 7); "I am in distress . . . sorrow . . . grief" (vs. 9); "I am the utter contempt of my neighbors . . . a dread to my friends" (vs. 11); "I hear the slander of many" (vs. 13); "they conspire against me" (vs. 13); "I was in a besieged city" (vs. 21).

Step 3

After kids examine Psalm 31, have them stand in a circle, hold hands, and close their eyes. Ask each kid to use one word to identify one emotion that he or she felt during the past week. Have kids say their words in order around the circle. Ask a few volunteers to explain what events caused their emotions.

Step 4

Have kids pair up. Instruct them to choose an encouraging verse from "Emotions in Motion" (Repro Resource 2) or any passage in the Bible to write out and present to their partners. Then have the partners pray for each other, thanking God for being available to comfort and help us with our emotions. Before they pray, they might ask their partner for specific prayer requests concerning struggles the partner may be having in the area of emotions. Challenge kids to pray for their partners during the week.

MOSTLY **GIRLS**

MOSTLY **GUYS**

EXTRA **FUN**

Step 3
After completing "Emotions in Motion" (Repro Resource 2), ask your group members to respond to the following statement: **Many people say that girls are more emotional than guys, so how could David write a psalm like this one?** You might also ask your group members to comment on the statements listed in the "Mostly Guys" option for Step 4, adding one final question:
(6) If guys had to deal with PMS and other woman-stuff, they'd be more emotional.

Step 4
Talk about Psalm 31:1 and God's power to keep us from "being put to shame" or embarrassed. Ask: **What are some ways our changing emotions can embarrass us? How do you handle embarrassing situations? What could you do to help you remember to pray for God's help when you need more self-control with your emotions?**

Step 2
Guys will probably enjoy an opportunity to move around the room. They might also enjoy an added challenge. After group members move to the appropriate part of the room in response to each question, let one volunteer challenge someone else who is standing nearby. He should say something like this: "I think that my lunch today was better (or worse) than yours." Then the two have to describe their lunches. The rest of the group will decide whose lunch was better (or worse).

Step 4
If you're not sure how the balloon activity will go over with your group, give a short true-false test.
**(1) Real men don't cry.
(2) Guys aren't as emotional as girls.
(3) It's not cool to show too much emotion.
(4) If you're angry, it's better to explode and get it off your chest than to let it eat you up inside.
(5) It's hard for most guys to talk about their emotions.**
  After giving the test, discuss each answer in more detail. Ask: **How do you think David would have answered this question? Why?**

Step 1
Before the session begins, have a "Roller Coaster of Emotions" contest. Invite daring volunteers to sign up for these contests: Screaming Meemies, Laugh 'Til You're Sick, and Real Tears. You might want to limit the sign-ups to three people per contest. Announce the contests like a game show host. **Do you scream well? Well enough to make someone's blood curdle? Then here's your chance to sign up for the Screaming Meemies contest. The winner will receive a fantastic, wonderful, amazing, fabulous, incredible candy bar.** Figure out how to decide on the winners. Award small prizes in categories like the most unusual scream (not necessarily the loudest), the funniest laugh, and the most convincing tears. Then move on to the rest of Step 1 as it's written.

Step 4
Balloons are always more fun when they're filled with helium. Rent a helium tank from a party shop and let kids take home helium-filled balloons (with Scripture verses taped to the balloon string). You may also want to buy higher quality balloons that will last a while and festive ribbon instead of string. Or buy balloons in unusual colors or with encouraging messages preprinted on them. You may also want to buy more than one balloon for each kid.

Step 1

Create a powerful presentation by videotaping the expression of a series of opposite emotions back-to-back. Scan your television guide for programs that might be good sources. Or get ideas from your own video library or a friend's. For example, tape a scene of a joyful, frenzied audience at a rock concert followed by a scene of a single, weeping person. Or tape a news story that shows an angry, screaming mob followed by a scene in which a mother is gently singing to her baby. Or show a scene in which someone is screaming at his or her spouse followed by a scene of a big brother gently pushing a little brother in a swing. Or show a war scene followed by a comedy routine. Use this video to kick off the session. Have kids identify the emotions they saw. Then move into Step 1.

Step 4

Close the session in a lighthearted way. Bring in a supermarket tabloid and have kids react as you read some of the headlines aloud. Read through a couple of the stories that most interest kids. Skip the questionable stuff. Talk about the emotions that kids felt as they listened to the headlines.

Step 1

If you are short on time, skip the balloon activity in Step 1. Just ask the first two questions from Step 1; then go right into Step 2. This way, kids won't miss the brief review of the last session, which is brought out in Step 1. And Step 2 is lighthearted enough to give them time to warm up to the idea of discussing "emotions."

Step 4

If you are short on time, don't skip reading Psalm 31 aloud during Step 3. It will be good for kids to read Scripture together as a group after they've worked on it in pairs. Instead, you can save time in Step 4 by having the balloons already blown up with strings attached. Then all kids have to do is find an appropriate verse, write it down, and tape it to the balloon.

Step 1

Use the following option to illustrate how we should control our emotions. Blow up two balloons. On one of the balloons, tape an "X" with two pieces of transparent tape. Stick a pin in the untaped balloon. Of course, it will pop. Then, with the taped balloon, stick the pin *straight* into the crossed section of the tape and through the balloon's skin. If the tape is firm, with no air bubbles, the balloon will not pop. (Have other balloons ready just in case!) Let group members observe that it isn't a trick. Then pull the pin out *slowly* and watch the balloon. The air will slowly leak out of the balloon. Afterward, draw parallels, helping kids recognize that the force (emotion) pent up in the balloon (us), when protected by the tape (Holy Spirit), is able to be released in a calm and directed manner (self-control).

Step 4

Distribute one balloon and a slip of paper to each group member. Instruct kids to write down some specific steps they could take toward resolving one emotional issue. The steps should be practical enough that they could be accomplished in the next few days. Then have each kid fold his or her paper, stuff it into the balloon, blow up the balloon, and tie it tight. Say: **Before this balloon deflates, you must keep your promise and take the steps toward resolving your emotional issue.**

Step I

As much as possible, try to have a balanced mix of junior highers and high schoolers on the teams. High schoolers will probably be a little more comfortable with this activity because it requires more creativity and an ability to translate emotions into an unusual object lesson. Working alongside high schoolers should help junior highers feel more comfortable during the brainstorming and presentation of the stories.

Step 2

If your junior highers tend to hold back to see what your high schoolers do, you'll need to handle the regular activity differently. Instead of having kids move from one side of the room to the other to answer questions, pair them up with someone their own age. Then they can privately share their responses to your questions with their partner. They can go into more detail by talking, rather than only moving around the room. And they may feel freer to talk about their struggles, rather than trying to appear positive to a roomful of people.

Step 3

Have your sixth graders work in teams of three or four on "Emotions in Motion" (Repro Resource 2). As they are marking the different kinds of emotions, ask the teams also to choose one of the emotions to describe to the rest of the group and tell of a time when that emotion might be present. Ask: **What are some other ways, besides writing a psalm, that we can express our emotions to God?**

Step 4

If some of your sixth graders aren't sure which emotion they want God's help with, suggest that they write down Psalm 31:14. Talk about why God is worthy of our trust and how His unchanging character and unconditional love is a good example to follow, especially when our emotions are unpredictable. Ask some of the following questions to wrap up the session:

• **As you get older, is it getting easier or harder to handle your emotions? Why?**
• **At what age do you think people are best able to handle their emotions? Why?**
• **Some people say the teen years are an emotional roller coaster. From what you've seen so far, do you think they're right?**
• **What fears do you have about being a teenager?**

Date Used:

Approx.
Time

Step 1: A Lot of Hot Air _____
o Small Group
o Large Group
o Extra Fun
o Media
o Short Meeting Time
o Urban
o Combined Junior High/High School
Things needed:

Step 2: Say What You Feel_____
o Small Group
o Mostly Guys
o Combined Junior High/High School
Things needed:

Step 3: Emotional Rescue _____
o Extra Action
o Large Group
o Heard It All Before
o Little Bible Background
o Fellowship & Worship
o Mostly Girls
o Sixth Grade
Things needed:

Step 4: Help from a Friend_____
o Extra Action
o Heard It All Before
o Little Bible Background
o Fellowship & Worship
o Mostly Girls
o Mostly Guys
o Extra Fun
o Media
o Short Meeting Time
o Urban
o Sixth Grade
Things needed:

3 What to Do with Anger

CRACK!!

YOUR GOALS FOR THIS SESSION:

Choose one or more

☐ To help kids discover that anger is not necessarily a negative emotion.

☐ To help kids understand that there are God-honoring ways to express anger and sinful ways to express anger.

☐ To help kids choose healthy, God-honoring ways to deal with their anger.

☐ Other _____

Your Bible Base:

Matthew 18:15-17
Ephesians 4:26-30

Sticky Emotions

(Needed: Name tags with different emotions written on them)

Before the session, you'll need to prepare several name tags (one for each group member) by writing a different emotion on each one. Among the emotions you might use are happiness, sadness, anger, fear, jealousy, disappointment, hatred, and revenge. If you have a large group, it's OK to use an emotion more than once.

As group members arrive, stick a name tag on the back of each person. Make sure group members can't see what's written on their name tags.

Say: **Each of you is wearing a name tag with a specific emotion written on it. Your job is to find out what your emotion is. To do this, you'll have to pay attention to the way the other people in the group talk to you.**

Explain that when you give the signal, everyone will "mingle" for a few minutes. However, as kids mingle, they must communicate with each other only in ways that illustrate the emotions on each other's name tags. For instance, if you saw someone with a "jealousy" name tag, you might walk up and say, "I wish *I* had that shirt you're wearing. You *always* get all of the nicest clothes." Or if you saw someone with a "revenge" name tag, you might walk up and say, "I'll get you back for what you did to me if it's the last thing I ever do!"

Encourage group members to keep their comments to each other brief—perhaps one or two sentences—and not to be so obvious that the other person figures out his or her emotion right away. If you want to make it more challenging, don't allow any talking. Kids should only communicate nonverbally. After a person guesses his or her emotion, he or she may remove the name tag. Continue until everyone has guessed his or her emotion.

Afterward, say: **We've got a lot of different emotions represented here on these name tags. But today we're going to focus on one in particular—anger.**

Have those group members whose name tag said "anger" come to the front of the room for a brief contest. You may also want to ask for a couple of other volunteers to compete. The object of the game is to see who can pretend to be angriest. Each contestant will have 15 seconds to demonstrate anger through facial expressions, tone of voice, body language, etc. (You may want to emphasize that contestants may not use swearing or personal verbal attacks in their "performances.")

After all of the contestants have performed, vote as a group on which one was the angriest. Then bestow on that person the title "King/Queen of Anger."

A Different Look at Anger

(Needed: Copies of Repro Resource 3, pencils)

Have group members form pairs. Distribute copies of "Abstract Anger" (Repro Resource 3) and pencils to each pair.

Explain: **Use your imagination to answer these questions about anger. Of course, there are no right or wrong answers. We just want to see what kinds of things you associate with anger.**

Give the pairs a few minutes to work. When everyone is finished, go through the questions one at a time and have each pair share its response.

Use the following responses to supplement the pairs' answers.

(1) If anger were a color, what color would it be? (Red or hot pink.)

(2) If anger were a car, what kind of car would it be? (A black hot rod with flames painted on the sides.)

(3) If anger were a shoe, what kind of shoe would it be? (A motorcycle boot with spurs on it.)

(4) If anger were a song, what song would it be? (A heavy metal song with lyrics about death and destruction.)

(5) If anger were a dog, what kind of dog would it be? (A pit bull.)

(6) If anger were a sound, what sound would it be? (An exploding firecracker.)

(7) If anger were an odor, what odor would it be? (Burning rubber.)

(8) If anger were a food, what food would it be? (Jalapeño peppers.)

(9) If anger were a liquid, what liquid would it be? (Hot lava spewing from a volcano.)

(10) If anger were weather, what kind of weather would it be? (A lightning storm.)

Afterward, say: **True or false: Anger is a bad emotion.** Get responses from as many group members as possible.

Have someone read aloud the first six words of Ephesians 4:26 ("In your anger do not sin").

OPTIONS

LARGE GROUP

HEARD IT ALL BEFORE

LITTLE BIBLE BACKGROUND

MOSTLY GUYS

EXTRA FUN

MEDIA

JR. HIGH / HIGH SCHOOL COMBINED

Ask: **If anger were a bad emotion, what would this verse have said?** (Do not get angry.)

Explain: **Ephesians 4:26 tells us not to sin in our anger. That means it's possible to be angry without sinning. So anger is not necessarily a bad emotion. How you _express_ your anger determines whether it's good or bad.**

STEP 3

Anger in Action

(Needed: Copies of Repro Resource 4, Bibles)

Distribute copies of "Anger: Up Close and Personal" (Repro Resource 4). Explain: **Here are two anger-causing situations. Let's take a look at them and see if we can come up with some positive and some negative ways to respond to them.**

Give group members a minute or two to read the first situation. Then say: **I'm going to read a list of possible responses to this situation. If you think a response is positive, give me a thumbs-up sign. If you think a response is negative, give me a thumbs-down sign. If you're not sure, shrug your shoulders.**

The possible responses are as follows:
• Spread a rumor that Sara cheated on the math test, but was so dumb she still only got a "C–."
• Spray-paint "LIAR" in big letters on the side of Sara's house.
• Tell Richard, the guy Sara's madly in love with, about the time Sara threw up in the middle of McDonald's.
• Trip Sara as she's walking down the hall.
• Don't ever mention the incident to Sara; just deal with it privately.

If no one mentions it, point out that all five responses are negative. The first four are based on revenge. Anger becomes sin when it causes you to do things to "get even" with someone else. The fifth response involves suppressing anger. When anger is not dealt with properly, it can cause some serious problems later.

Have someone read aloud Matthew 18:15-17. Then ask: **According to this passage, what is the first thing you should do when someone makes you angry or hurts you?** (Go and talk to the person one-on-one. Explain to the person how you feel and why you're so angry or upset.)

What might happen if Mary talked to Sara one-on-one

OPTIONS

EXTRA ACTION

HEARD IT ALL BEFORE

LITTLE BIBLE BACKGROUND

FELLOWSHIP & WORSHIP

MOSTLY GIRLS

MOSTLY GUYS

MEDIA

SHORT MEETING TIME

URBAN

SIXTH GRADE

about how she's feeling? (Sara might realize how much she hurt Mary, apologize, and admit her lie to Mr. Reed and the other kids in the math class. Sara might also explain to Mary why she did what she did. She might have had some resentment toward Mary that had been growing for some time. In a one-on-one setting, the two of them might be able to work things out. It's possible that Sara won't apologize, but at least Mary took the initiative to make things right.)

Give group members a minute or two to read the second situation on Repro Resource 4. Then ask: **Do you think Jason has a right to be angry in this situation?** (Yes. He was falsely accused and punished for something he didn't do.)

Put yourself in Jason's position. Let's say your mother, after she realized her mistake, came to you crying and apologizing for what she did. What would be some negative ways you might respond to the situation? (Yell at your mother for ruining your weekend; refuse to speak to her for several days; keep reminding her of the incident to make her feel bad; demand that she do special things for you to make up for her mistake; etc.)

Have someone read aloud Ephesians 4:26-30. Then ask: **According to this passage, what should we *not* do when someone makes us angry?** (Allow our anger to last more than a day without resolving it; give the devil a chance to take advantage of our anger; talk "unwholesomely" about the person who made us angry.)

Based on this passage, what should Jason do with his anger toward his mother? (Talk to her about how angry he is; resolve the situation before he goes to bed that night; avoid yelling or being sarcastic to his mother when he talks to her; etc.)

How could the devil get a "foothold" in this situation? What might happen if he did? (If Jason decided to sulk and stay mad at his mother for several days, the devil could cause Jason to doubt whether his mother really cares about him. That might lead to a *serious* relationship problem between Jason and his mother.)

STEP
4

Dealing with Anger

(Needed: Balloons, straight pin)

Quickly blow up a balloon and hold it by the nozzle. Explain: **There are several different ways to deal with anger. One way is to**

throw a fit or go into a rage. Let go of the balloon's nozzle, and send the balloon flying through the air.

Blow up another balloon and hold it by the nozzle. Say: **Another way to deal with anger is to gripe or complain to others.** Pinch the nozzle as you let the air out of the balloon, so that the escaping air makes a squealing noise.

Blow up the balloon and tie a knot in it. Say: **Another way to deal with anger is to hold it in.**

And another way to deal with anger is to explode. Quickly pop the balloon with a pin.

But none of these ways is really helpful. In fact, these methods might cause your anger to turn into sin.

Refer your group members back to Matthew 18:15-17 and Ephesians 4:26-30. Explain: **God tells us that when we're angry with someone, we should go to that person as quickly as possible and talk with him or her one-on-one. We should tell that person exactly how we feel—without using "unwholesome" talk—and work to straighten out the situation. I know it's harder than it sounds, especially when we're angry. But we have God's Word on it that it's the best way to deal with our anger.**

Blow up another balloon. Say: **A minute ago we looked at some negative ways to deal with anger. A more constructive way is to keep your cool, but take whatever steps are necessary to deal with it.** Slowly let the air out, while keeping control of the balloon.

Instruct group members to think of someone they're angry with now or have been angry with recently. Have them consider how they can use the principles in Matthew 18 and Ephesians 4 to resolve the situation. If time permits, ask for a couple of volunteers to share what they plan to do.

Close the session in prayer, asking God to help your group members resolve their anger in ways that are pleasing to Him.

As group members leave, distribute uninflated balloons to help remind them not to deal with their anger in negative ways.

Abstract Anger

1. If anger were a color, what color would it be?

2. If anger were a car, what kind of car would it be?

3. If anger were a shoe, what kind of shoe would it be?

4. If anger were a song, what song would it be?

5. If anger were a dog, what kind of dog would it be?

6. If anger were a sound, what sound would it be?

7. If anger were an odor, what odor would it be?

8. If anger were a food, what food would it be?

9. If anger were a liquid, what liquid would it be?

10. If anger were weather, what kind of weather would it be?

Anger: Up Close and Personal

Situation #1

Sara and Mary *used* to be good friends. They played on the junior high tennis team together; they were counselors at summer camp together; and they often studied together. In fact, last week Mary stayed at Sara's house for the entire weekend so the two of them could study for Monday's big math test. (It counted as one-third of the final semester grade.)

On Wednesday, Mr. Reed handed back the tests. Mary got an "A-"; Sara got a "C-." Mary was excited that she'd done so well, but she felt bad for Sara. She tried to talk to Sara after class, but Sara didn't seem to want to talk.

The next day in the cafeteria, Mary overheard a couple of guys from her math class talking about her.

"I always thought she was real straightlaced. I never thought she'd do something like that," one of them said.

"It was probably just an act," another one said. "She knew no one would suspect her, so she could get away with it."

Mary was confused. She couldn't figure out what they were talking about. A few minutes later, Mary ran into Sara and a couple of other girls in the hall. She told them about what she'd heard in the cafeteria.

"Oh, quit pretending, Mary," Sara said disgustedly. "You know you cheated on the math test. So I made sure that everyone else knows—including Mr. Reed. If I were you, I wouldn't get too excited about that 'A-'—if you know what I mean."

Sara and her friends laughed as they walked away. Mary couldn't believe it. Sara was telling people that Mary had cheated on the math test, when she knew it wasn't true. Some friend! Sara was spreading lies about Mary, and those lies were about to get Mary in trouble!

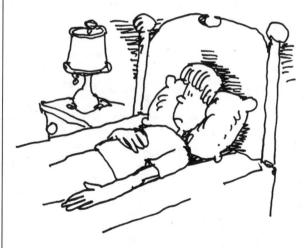

Situation #2

On Thursday morning, Jason's mother discovered five dollars missing from her purse. When Jason's brother, Matt, came home from school for lunch, his mother asked him if he knew anything about the missing money.

"No," Matt said, "but I saw Jason in your room this morning. Maybe he knows something about it."

When Jason got home from school that afternoon, his mother cornered him in the living room.

"Were you in my purse this morning?" she demanded.

"No, I don't think so," Jason said slowly, trying to remember.

"Your brother said he saw you in my room this morning. What were you doing there?" his mother asked.

"Oh, yeah, that's right!" Jason said, suddenly remembering. "I was looking for a pen for school."

"And you just happened to find five dollars instead, right?" his mother added.

"I didn't take any money, Mom," Jason said.

"Don't make things worse by lying!" his mom warned. "You're grounded to your room for the weekend."

"But, Mom, I—" he started.

"Do you want me to make it two weekends?" she threatened.

Jason stopped arguing and went to his room. Over the weekend, he missed his park-district baseball game, going to see the Cubs with one of his friends, and his favorite TV show. It was one of the longest weekends of Jason's life.

Monday morning, as Jason's mom was getting ready for work, she reached for her new pair of earrings. Suddenly she remembered that she'd used the five dollars in her purse to buy the earrings.

EXTRA ACTION

SMALL GROUP

LARGE GROUP

Step 1

Instead of having only a few kids participate in the "show anger" contest, have everyone take part. Bring an instant camera and enough film to take two pictures of each group member pretending to be angry. Let kids take home one of their own pictures to remind them of the session. Provide poster board or newsprint, markers, tape or glue, scissors, etc., so the kids can create a huge poster about anger. Include the remaining photos on the poster. Display the poster for a couple of weeks.

Step 3

As you describe the five ways Mary might respond in anger to Sara, list the responses on the board. Also list the responses kids come up with for Situation 2. Then have two volunteers roleplay an ending for Situation 1. They can get an idea of possible responses from the list on the board. Tell them to keep acting until you say **Freeze!** (Give them about 15-30 seconds.) Then let the actors choose replacements to roleplay a different ending to the skit. Say **Freeze!** again, and so on. Let several kids do this with Situation 2 also. Then have a couple of kids read Matthew 18:15-17 and Ephesians 4:26-30 aloud. Discuss the principles these verses teach on handling our anger. Have more volunteers act out endings to both situations based on these scriptural guidelines.

Step 1

If you don't have enough kids to make the name-tag game fun, you may want to use another idea to loosen kids up at the beginning of the session. Pass around a twelve-inch ruler, a pair of scissors, and a ball of string. Have each person cut off a foot-long section of string. One at a time, kids should wrap the string around their index finger. With each wrap, they should "fess up" about a time when they lost their temper.

Step 4

Have kids debate whether they would be able to control their anger for the rest of their lives if they were paid $1,000,000 to do it. Let them define limitations for themselves. Would they never be allowed to glare, yell, scream, swear, etc? Or would it be OK to glare? What if they had to pay back the money if they even just felt angry inside? (A microchip slipped under their skin would alert the authorities to angry feelings.) Find out how much group members picked up in this session by asking them to write down the reference to one of the session's Bible passages on anger. Also have them write down one way in which God wants them to deal with their anger.

Step 2

Have the group create a huge mural to fill a wall in the room. Base the mural on the comparisons they came up with. ("If anger were a _____, what would it be?") Provide poster board or newsprint, markers, scissors, magazines, etc. for the project.

Step 4

The object lesson with balloons will be more effective in a large group if you get the kids involved. If it won't break your budget, give each kid a balloon. It's best if the balloons are all the same size. Have kids perform the following activities in groups of eight to ten.

• When demonstrating fits of rage, have each kid blow up his or her balloon, stand behind a certain line, and let the balloon go. The balloon that goes farthest wins.

• When demonstrating griping or complaining, see which kid can make the longest continuous noise by pinching his or her balloon nozzle and letting the air out.

• When demonstrating holding anger in, have each kid tie his or her balloon in a knot. He or she should then kick the balloon, alternating feet (left foot, right foot, left foot, etc.). See who can keep his or her balloon off the floor the longest. Throw in some more difficult actions like off the head, backward kick, or kicking with both feet while laying on the floor.

• When demonstrating exploding, have a group countdown, starting at ten. When you say **Blast-off!** have the kids pop their balloons at the very same moment.

• After reviewing the Scripture passages, give each kid one more balloon to blow up. He or she should then slowly let the air out of the balloon. The person can then take this balloon home as a reminder of how to deal with anger constructively.

HEARD IT ALL BEFORE

LITTLE BIBLE BACKGROUND

FELLOWSHIP & WORSHIP

Step 2

Even kids who think they've heard it all before may discover something new about themselves as a result of the following activity. Prepare and copy a list of general situations that could evoke anger. Give each kid a copy. Have kids check off the situations that have made them angry in the past. They might be shocked at how many they check off. Here are some examples: being teased by a brother or sister, having to do a chore, being punished, stubbing a toe, getting a poor grade, missing the bus, waiting for someone who is late, etc. Have kids place a star next to the items that have angered them more than once. Then have them circle one item that upsets them the most. After a few minutes, have them share their responses.

Step 3

If some kids think that anger is no big deal, skip Repro Resource 4. Instead, read the following excerpt from *Gifted Hands* by Dr. Ben Carson, a Christian pediatric surgeon. **"I was in the ninth grade when the unthinkable happened. I lost control and tried to knife a friend. [They were arguing about what radio station to listen to.] In that instant blind anger—pathological anger— took possession of me. Grabbing the camping knife I carried in my back pocket, I snapped it open and lunged for the boy who had been my friend. With all the power of my young muscles, I thrust the knife toward his belly."** Fortunately, the knife hit his friend's big, heavy buckle, saving his life. Carson could not believe that he almost killed his friend. Generally, Carson was pretty patient, but once he got angry, he would go crazy. After this incident, Carson asked God to take control of his temper. He has learned to appropriately express his anger, despite all kinds of stress in his life. Ask: **Do you know anyone who might be capable of this kind of rage? Have you ever felt that you might go out of control with anger?**

Step 2

Point out that God gets angry too. Ask volunteers to read the following passages as you take a look at various facets of God's anger: Psalm 2:12; 30:5; 78:38; Numbers 14:18; Deuteronomy 29:26-28. Then ask: **How do these passages describe God's anger? What makes God angry? How is our anger like or unlike God's?**

Step 3

If kids can't figure out what some of the phrases in Matthew 18:15-17 and Ephesians 4:26-30 mean, offer the following explanations.

• "Treat him as you would a pagan or a tax collector"—Jews did not think very highly of pagans (Gentiles) or tax collectors, even though both kinds of people were being saved and were shown compassion by Jesus.

• "Do not give the devil a foothold"— When we don't deal with our anger properly, Satan can use it to create bigger problems.

• "Unwholesome talk"—Hurtful comments, as opposed to encouraging words.

• "Do not grieve the Holy Spirit of God"—When Christians sin, the Holy Spirit who lives in us is saddened. Sin interferes with His purpose in our lives, which is to set us apart for God.

• "Sealed for the day of redemption"— This gives us hope to "hang in there" with God until the day that He has chosen to come for us.

Step 3

Instead of using Repro Resource 4, invite a visitor (preferably someone from your church that your kids know) to explain his or her struggle with anger and how he or she learned to rely on God for help in dealing with it. Encourage the speaker to quote or read Scripture that applies to the situation. Afterward, let kids ask questions. Invite kids to describe similar struggles in their own lives and to pray for one another. To do so, you might have them form groups of three to complete the following statements:

• "I'm most angry when . . ."
• "The last time I was angry, I . . ."

Step 4

Here is a good way to get kids to pray for each other about controlling their anger. Give each person a candle. Then have kids sit in a circle in a darkened room (or go outside if it's dark). Explain that you will light the first person's candle. He or she will then pray for someone else in the circle, and then light that person's candle. That person will then pray for someone else, and so on, until everyone in the group has been prayed for. Point out that the candle represents God's light in our lives and His willingness to help us control our anger.

Step 3

Before distributing "Anger: Up Close and Personal" (Repro Resource 4), ask for some volunteers to act out the situations on the sheet. If possible, get at least five or six volunteers for Situation #1 (with some of the kids playing friends of the main characters). Get three volunteers for Situation #2. (You may need to change names from Jason to Janet and from Matt to Martha.) Ask the volunteers to adjust the events in the situation as they wish. Provide a little planning time; then have the volunteers present the skits. Ask the entire group to contribute to the discussion at the end of each presentation.

Step 4

As a group, talk about what to do when others around you are angry. Say: **Often we aren't angry until someone responds to us in anger—then we pick up their anger. What do you usually do? What should you do? How would you respond if the following people were really angry?**
- **Friends**
- **Parents**
- **Brothers or sisters**
- **Someone that's hard to like**
- **Teachers**
- **A person you'd like to be friends with**

Step 2

When your guys give their answers to the questions from Repro Resource 3, have them sound as angry and mean as possible—just for fun. Also encourage them to create sound effects whenever possible instead of giving their answers straight. Have the rest of the group try to guess what the answer is based on the sound effect.

Step 3

Have cans of all kinds of soda on hand. Let two contestants compete to create the loudest burp. Let them choose their sodas, pour equal amounts into glasses of the same size, guzzle, and burp away. Take a vote on the best burp. Then let two more contestants compete. (Open new cans every time.) You may want to give out small prizes to the winners. Draw parallels between burps and anger. Point out that sometimes it is hard to suppress a burp when it really wants to come out. If you don't let it out, you feel uncomfortable. Talk about how uncomfortable it can feel to keep anger bottled up inside. Discuss appropriate and inappropriate ways for letting anger out.

Another good object lesson using soda is to let kids shake up cans and see who can create the biggest explosion upon opening them. This is a lot like people who keep their anger bottled up inside. If you use an object lesson like this, you can skip the balloon activities in Step 4 and spend your time cleaning up!

Step 2

Have kids form teams of three for a "toilet paper nose relay." Appoint one team member to be an "enemy," another to be a "friend," and the third to be a "contestant." The enemy is to try to prevent his or her "teammates" from winning the relay. The friend is to offer encouragement and advice during the relay. The contestant will actually compete. Give each team a roll of toilet paper. Designate a finish line on the other side of the room. When you blow the whistle, the contestant on each team should roll the paper toward the finish line with his or her nose. The first team to reach the finish line wins. During play, the "enemy" should discourage the other two players by contradicting instructions and encouragement given by the "friendly" teammate, blocking the view, making noise, etc. No one is allowed to touch anyone else or to stop the contestant from rolling the toilet paper. Award a prize to the winning toilet paper roller and the "friend" on his or her team. Afterward, have kids talk about whether they felt angry at any point during or after the game, and why.

Step 4

Have two teams compete to see which can make the most popcorn in ten minutes. If you can't borrow air poppers that are exactly alike (so the competition is fair), and if you have access to a stove, give each team a pot, plenty of oil and popping corn, and a few large paper sacks to put the popped corn in. Award prizes to the winners if you want. While kids eat the popcorn, discuss parallels between the popping corn and anger. There are two analogies you could make: (1) Some of the kernels did not "explode," despite the hot oil. Compare this to controlling one's temper. (2) Some of the kernels never popped, so they're no good to eat. Compare this to people who don't deal with their anger. Have kids describe what it's like to be around a person with a bad temper and a person with a good temper.

Step 2

Follow up your last statement in Step 2 with the following activity. Bring in current newspapers or newsmagazines. Have kids cut out and discuss stories that involve anger. Ask: **What is this story about? What role do you think anger played in it? How could this problem have been averted if the anger had been dealt with according to the guidelines found in Matthew 18:15-17 and Ephesians 4:26-30?**

Step 3

If some of your kids are heavy metal or grunge fans, you could borrow almost any tape or CD they have, and find songs with a theme related to anger or its by-product—hate. During the session, play excerpts from a song or two. If you can, type up the lyrics for the excerpts you use and display them on an overhead projector. You could also do a little research on the lifestyles of the band members. (For information, you might check *The Guide to Periodical Literature* at your local library.) Ask: **What message does this band/person/song communicate? How does this message oppose the guidelines for dealing with anger that are given in Matthew 18:15-17 and Ephesians 4:26-30?**

Step 1

To save some time, skip the name-tag contest and go right to the contest in which kids compete to see who can act angriest. You may have to throw out a few challenges to inspire volunteers. Say: **I need a couple of people who are in the mood to do something crazy— people who are willing to do this crazy thing in front of the whole group. If you do this crazy thing the best, you'll (a) win a prize, (b) have the respect of the whole group, or (c) look weird.**

Step 3

Have students look up Matthew 21:1-13. Instruct them to reenact the scene from verses 12 and 13. You could provide props like a plastic "kiddy" table, stuffed animals, play money, etc. Students should mingle about, barter, and eat food that was "bought" with the play money. After Jesus clears the temple and the money changers react, bring the group together. Ask: **What triggered Jesus' anger? When is it appropriate to get angry? Was Jesus' response appropriate?** Ask various students how they felt as they played their parts—Jesus, sellers, buyers, innocent bystanders, etc.

Step 3

Have group members form two to four teams. Instruct the members of each team to discuss responses to the following situations, focusing on how anger might be expressed in a positive way and in a negative way for each situation.

(1) You were just slapped in the face by someone who hates you.
(2) You found out that the person who set your apartment building on fire is in your class.
(3) You keep getting teased that you're gay because you like ballet (if you're a guy) or sports (if you're a girl).
(4) You know the person who spray-painted a racial slur on your locker.

After group members discuss these situations, point out that anger is an emotion that helps make us aware of injustice and move us to action. Ask: **What are some things that happen in the city that are unjust and make you angry?** List responses as they are given, and discuss how some of them could be acted upon.

Step 4

The best way to deal with anger caused by others is to learn how to confront those people lovingly. Distribute paper and pens. Challenge kids to write down three starting phrases that can help them lovingly confront someone who has angered them. Examples might include "May I speak with you privately?" or "There's something I'd like to talk with you about." Point out that sometimes love needs to be tough, so the statements shouldn't let people off the hook too easily. For example, the following statement wouldn't be effective: "I'm sorry you tried to burn down my apartment building. But hey, that's OK. We all have our little faults."

PLANNING CHECKLIST

Step 2

The following activity is a good way to get kids of different ages to interact. Have each person write out a question he or she has about dealing with anger. The question should involve a personal struggle. Collect the questions and mix them up (keeping them anonymous). Then have group members form teams that include both junior highers and high schoolers. Give each team one or more of the questions. Each team must come up with an answer for its assigned question(s). Each answer must include a principle from the Bible. (For help, the teams could look up "anger" or "angry" in a Bible concordance.) When everyone is ready, have each team read its question(s) and share its answer(s).

Step 4

Invite people with different physical or mental disabilities to talk to the group about their frustrations and how they try to deal with them. After each presentation, let kids ask questions. Then talk about how out-of-control anger can be a disability. Follow up with the discussion in Step 4.

Step 3

As a group, discuss "Anger: Up Close and Personal" (Repro Resource 4). Then ask for suggestions of other situations that make people angry. Ask for volunteers to act out the situations, demonstrating both inappropriate and appropriate responses. Afterward, have other kids comment on what they might do in similar situations.

Step 4

Have your sixth graders form teams. Give each team a gummy worm; a rubber band; a short, strong wooden or aluminum rod; a braided cord; a lightweight plastic bucket with a handle; and a brick. Have each team conduct an experiment. Instruct each team to put the brick in the bucket and try to hang the bucket from each item, beginning with the gummy worm. After kids conduct their experiments, have them talk about the result of each one. Then ask how they think each test relates to anger. (Explain that the brick in the bucket represents anger and the rest of the objects represent ways we deal with anger.) Help kids see that a gummy worm will always give in to the weight of anger; a rubber band might bear the weight for a moment, until it snaps; a rod and a cord can both bear the weight of anger (although a cord is more flexible than a rod). Ask: **Which of these objects best describes how you deal with anger?**

After the object lesson, write the principles from Matthew 18:15-17 and Ephesians 4:26-30 on the board. Then ask: **When are these guidelines hard to follow? How can your relationship with God help make doing these things easier?**

Date Used:

Approx. Time

Step 1: Sticky Emotions _____
o Extra Action
o Small Group
o Short Meeting Time
Things needed:

Step 2: A Different Look at Anger _____
o Large Group
o Heard It All Before
o Little Bible Background
o Mostly Guys
o Extra Fun
o Media
o Combined Junior High/High School
Things needed:

Step 3: Anger in Action _____
o Extra Action
o Heard It All Before
o Little Bible Background
o Fellowship & Worship
o Mostly Girls
o Mostly Guys
o Media
o Short Meeting Time
o Urban
o Sixth Grade
Things needed:

Step 4: Dealing with Anger _____
o Small Group
o Large Group
o Fellowship & Worship
o Mostly Girls
o Extra Fun
o Urban
o Combined Junior High/High School
o Sixth Grade
Things needed:

How Can I Feel Better?

YOUR GOALS FOR THIS SESSION:

Choose one or more

☐ To help kids recognize that seeking happiness through artificial means (things like alcohol, drugs, sex, and food) is a bad idea.

☐ To help kids understand how to find real happiness, based on principles from God's Word.

☐ To help kids choose creative, God-honoring ways to help themselves feel better when things aren't going so great.

☐ Other _____
_____

Your Bible Base:

Psalm 100

Always Read the Instructions

(Needed: Copies of Repro Resource 5, pencils, prize)

To begin the session, distribute copies of "No Shortcuts, Please" (Repro Resource 5) and pencils. Place the sheets facedown in front of group members as you pass them out.

Explain: **We're going to begin our session today with a brief quiz. When I say "Go," you will turn your papers over and follow the directions on the sheet. You may not talk with each other while you take the quiz, and you may not look at anyone else's sheet. As soon as you're finished, raise your hand. The first person to correctly complete the quiz will receive a prize. Ready, go!**

Walk around as group members work, paying attention to who follows the directions and who doesn't. Those who follow the directions will answer only numbers 2, 5, and 8. Award a prize (perhaps a candy bar) to the first person who answers these three questions. When other group members question or complain, refer them to number 20 on the sheet.

Afterward, ask: **How many of you took the "shortcut" and wrote your responses before you read all of the instructions?** Get a show of hands.

What are some other shortcuts that people take? (Drivers often take side streets and back roads as shortcuts to their destinations. Kids doing homework often take shortcuts by "half-answering" questions and by not checking their answers. Building contractors sometimes take shortcuts to save money by using inferior materials, ignoring safety guidelines, etc.)

Explain: **Sometimes when we take shortcuts, we think we're making things easier for ourselves. But shortcuts aren't always the best way. Today we're going to be talking about shortcuts that some people take to become "happy"; then we'll compare those shortcuts with God's way for us to be truly happy.**

STEP 2

Cookie Time

(Needed: Blindfolds, plastic spoons, homemade chocolate chip cookies, chalkboard and chalk or newsprint and marker, several plastic containers— each containing one ingredient for chocolate chip cookies)

OPTIONS

[NOTE: The following activity will require a little more preparation than most of the other activities in this book. If you don't have time to prepare, you can simply describe the gist of the object lesson. It won't be as effective as actually performing the activity, but it will still work.]

Before the session, you'll need to make (or have one of your group members make) a batch of chocolate chip cookies. You'll also need to bring in several plastic containers. Each one should contain an ingredient for chocolate chip cookies. Among the ingredients you might use are butter, sugar, brown sugar, vanilla, eggs, flour, baking soda, salt, and chocolate chips. [NOTE: It's important that you bring in only all-natural ingredients and that you use only all-natural ingredients when you make the cookies.]

Ask for three or four volunteers to participate in a "taste test." Blindfold the volunteers, and give each one a plastic spoon. Put each volunteer in front of a container. Instruct the volunteers to dip their spoons into the containers (you may need to guide them), taste what's inside, and then describe the taste to the rest of the group. Some of the ingredients—like the sugar and chocolate chips—will taste good. Others—like the flour and baking soda—will taste bad.

Lead the group in a round of applause for your brave volunteers, and then have the volunteers take their seats.

Explain: **The items in these containers are ingredients— ingredients for chocolate chip cookies. When you taste the ingredients on their own, some of them are pretty gross. However, when you mix the ingredients together, the results can be pretty tasty.** Pass out homemade chocolate chip cookies. (You might want to give extra cookies to your taste-test volunteers.)

As group members enjoy their cookies, say: **You could say that our lives are like these cookies—they're made up of ingredients. Some of the ingredients of our lives are good, and leave a sweet taste in our mouth. These would be the times when we're happy and enjoying life. Some of our lives' ingredients aren't so good, and leave a bitter taste in our mouth. These would be the times when we're depressed or sad, and not** enjoying life very much.

What would happen if you tried to make chocolate chip cookies without baking soda, or flour, or salt, or butter, or any of the other bad-tasting ingredients? (The cookies would be incomplete. They wouldn't turn out right.)

By the same token, what would our lives be like if we didn't have down times—times of depression or sadness? (Our lives would be incomplete.)

Summarize: **Of course, probably none of us have ever wished for depressing or sad times—even if they do make our lives complete. If we had our choice, most of us would probably choose to be happy all of the time.**

What are some things that make you happy? (Being with friends, laughing, watching TV, listening to music, participating in sports, etc.) List group members' responses on the board as they are named.

Shortcuts and Artificial Ingredients

(Needed: Chalkboard and chalk or newsprint and marker)

Draw another analogy from your cookie activity. Say: **We used only all-natural ingredients for our chocolate chip cookies. We didn't have to; we could have used imitation butter, imitation salt, artificial sweeteners, artificially flavored chocolate, etc. But what would that have done to the cookies?** (It might have made them taste strange—or at least not as good as they tasted otherwise.)

By the same token, some people use "artificial ingredients" in their lives. They try to take "shortcuts" to happiness. What are some shortcuts people take to try to find happiness? What artificial ingredients do they use to make themselves happy? (Alcohol, drugs, sex, the pursuit of money or material possessions, power, etc.) List these responses on the board as they are named.

Can these things really make a person happy? (Only temporarily. Their effects wear off after a short time. So the person must constantly be looking for new ways to make himself or herself happy.)

Do you know anyone who tries to find happiness through alcohol, drugs, sex, or any other artificial ways? Emphasize that you're not looking for people's names here. **Do these people seem truly happy?** Get a few responses.

STEP 4

Real Happiness

(Needed: Chalkboard and chalk or newsprint and marker, paper, pencils)

Say: **We've seen where we can find artificial happiness. But where can we find real happiness?** (In God's Word.)

Have someone read aloud Psalm 100. Then ask: **How would you describe this psalm?** (Happy, joyful, full of thanksgiving.)

What is the psalmist so happy about? (He knows that the Lord is good and that His love and faithfulness endure forever.)

What are some of the instructions the psalmist gives in this psalm? Have group members call them out to you while you write them on the board. Responses should include the following:
- "Shout for joy to the Lord" (vs. 1).
- "Worship the Lord with gladness" (vs. 2).
- "Come before him with joyful songs" (vs. 2).
- "Know that the Lord is God" (vs. 3).
- "Enter his gates with thanksgiving" (vs. 4).
- "Give thanks to him" (vs. 4).
- "Praise his name" (vs. 4).

Ask: **Do you think any of these instructions could be helpful to us when we're feeling down? If so, how?** You might want to have group members pair up and work together on these questions. Give the pairs a few minutes to discuss; then have each one share its responses.

Use the following information to supplement the pairs' responses.

• Shouting for joy to the Lord, worshiping Him, and praising His name involve thinking about His greatness. When we're depressed or sad, reflecting on what a great God we serve can cheer us up.

• Singing joyful songs (perhaps hymns or contemporary worship tunes) is another way to overcome depression or sadness.

• If we know that the Lord is God, we know He has the power to lift us out of our depression and sadness.

• Entering His gates with thanksgiving and giving thanks to Him involves thinking about all God has done for us. Reflecting on what He's done for us could cause us to begin to feel special and cared for, and

OPTIONS

EXTRA ACTION

SMALL GROUP

LARGE GROUP

HEARD IT ALL BEFORE

LITTLE BIBLE BACKGROUND

FELLOWSHIP & WORSHIP

MOSTLY GIRLS

MOSTLY GUYS

SHORT MEETING TIME

URBAN

SIXTH GRADE

could chase away our depression and sadness.

Distribute paper and pencils. Say: **Imagine that you have a close friend who's been feeling sad and depressed lately. Write this friend a brief letter to cheer him or her up. If possible, give your friend some advice, based on Psalm 100.**

Give group members a few minutes to work. When they're finished, ask volunteers to share what they wrote. You might want to write some of their suggestions on the board as they are named.

Feel-Better Remedies

(Needed: Slips of paper, pencils)

Say: **True or false: Being a Christian means never getting depressed or sad.** (False.)
True or false: When you're depressed or sad, the only good ways to help yourself feel better are to pray, read the Bible, and sing hymns. Get several responses.

Distribute slips of paper and pencils. Instruct group members to write down one or two things they do to cheer up when they're feeling sad or depressed. Encourage them to be honest in their responses. You're not looking for "religious" answers here. If group members cheer themselves up by watching TV, listening to music, eating, or even by getting drunk or high, they should say so. (You could encourage them to disguise their handwriting if it would make them feel more comfortable.)

Collect the slips, and then read each one aloud. After you read each one, have group members call out whether they think it's a good way or a bad way to cheer up. You may need to emphasize that things like watching TV, listening to music, eating, shopping, and goofing off with friends are not necessarily bad remedies for depression and sadness. Doing things that are fun is not an ungodly way to feel better.

Summarize: **The key is dependence. We shouldn't depend on food or music or even our friends to help us feel better when we're depressed. Our deepest dependence should be on God. These other things are simply diversions. When we're sad or depressed, the first thing we should do is take our feelings to God in prayer and let Him help us.**

Close the session in prayer, thanking God that we can depend on Him to help us when we're feeling sad or depressed.

OPTIONS

LITTLE BIBLE BACKGROUND

FELLOWSHIP & WORSHIP

MOSTLY GIRLS

MOSTLY GUYS

MEDIA

JR. HIGH / HIGH SCHOOL COMBINED

REPRO RESOURCE
5

NO Short Cuts, *Please!*

Read each of the following instructions thoroughly. When you've finished reading all of the instructions, go back and write the appropriate responses.

1. Write your full name. _____

2. Write the age you'll be on your next birthday. _____

3. Write the first names of your brothers and sisters. _____

4. Write the names of the cities you've lived in. _____

5. Write the 26 letters of the alphabet in order. _____

6. Write the sum of 23 + 89. _____

7. Write the name of the last store you shopped in. _____

8. Write your address. _____

9. Write the name of your favorite cereal. _____

10. Write the name of your favorite rock group or singer. _____

11. Write your height. _____

12. Write the name of the holiday that falls on December 25. _____

13. Write your shoe size. _____

14. Write the name of your favorite teacher. _____

15. Write the name of your favorite radio station. _____

16. Write the name of your best friend. _____

17. Write the name of your favorite food. _____

18. Write the number of fingers you have. _____

19. Write the name of your favorite TV show. _____

20. Write nothing here. Now that you've read through all of the instructions, go back and answer only numbers 2, 5, and 8. _____

Step 1

Begin the session with a cheering contest. Have group members form teams. Instruct each team to come up with a cheer for God (or for your group). For example: "We love God! Yes we do! We love God! How 'bout you?!" or "Give me a 'G!' Give me an 'O!' Give me a 'D!' What's it spell? GOD! The one and only God of Abraham . . . Isaac . . . Jacob . . . and me!" Invite an impartial adult to pick the winner and runners-up. You may even want to award prizes. Afterward, talk about whether Christians should always be this cheerful. Ask: **If you get depressed, are you sinning?** Acknowledge that even the most mature Christians aren't always cheerful or happy—especially when life becomes difficult. But Christians can experience a quiet joy despite problems. If you wish, take a brief look at II Corinthians 1:8, in which Paul sounds anything but cheerful.

Step 4

Before you identify or read Psalm 100 in this step, have your kids do something a little crazy. Get five volunteers to stand in front of the group one at a time and spell out words in the air with their hips. (It will look hilarious.) Tell the group that the words are part of a psalm being written by someone who is feeling really happy. The rest of the group members should shout out each letter as they recognize it. Assign the following words: *shout, worship, sing, thank,* and *praise.* Then have kids read Psalm 100. Work through Step 4, beginning with the fourth question: **What are some of the instructions the psalmist gives in this psalm?**

Step 2

If your group is small, you could let everyone taste one or all of the separate ingredients that combine to make good cookies. That way, everyone will be able to personally relate to your comments about how sweet and bitter ingredients make one's life complete.

Step 4

If you have just a few kids, you may not want to have them work through Psalm 100 in pairs. Instead, you can have them answer this question from Step 4 as a group: **Do you think any of these instructions could be helpful to us when we're feeling down? If so, how?** Let kids call out their answers. Write them on the board as they are named. Since you have fewer kids, you will be able to spend more time listening to the letters they write to depressed friends. Also, group members will have more time to explain their friends' situations before they read their letters aloud.

Step 1

In a large group, the chances are pretty good that some of the kids will know the trick of Repro Resource 5 and not be fooled by it. Here's another alternative you might use: Pass out several vanilla wafers, or other "unexciting" cookies. Say: **You can have some of these now, or wait until later to have your snack.** Keep track of who takes cookies now. Exclude them from having any of the homemade cookies later in the session. Use this activity to talk about shortcuts people take to try to find happiness.

Step 4

Have group members form teams. Assign each team a different psalm. (You can still follow up with the questions in Step 4.) Here are some suggested psalms that are similar to Psalm 100: Psalm 103:1-5, 22; Psalm 105:1-5; Psalm 108:1-5; Psalm 113. Skip the letter-writing/advice-giving activity at the end of the step so that you have plenty of time for each team to read its psalm aloud and give its answers. Write these questions on the board so that kids know what to answer: **How would you describe this psalm? What is the psalmist so happy about? What are some of the instructions the psalmist gives in this psalm? Do you think any of these instructions could be helpful when we're feeling down? If so, how?**

Step 1

If your kids immediately figure out the gist of the shortcut trick from Repro Resource 5 or know it already, try another option. Give a volunteer a choice: he or she can have a candy bar that is sitting on top of an upside-down box or do ten sit-ups and get what might be a better prize under the box instead. The hidden prize should be better than the one in view. (It could be two candy bars.) No matter which choice the kid makes, you can lead into the discussion about shortcuts. If you want to involve the whole group, adapt the "Large Group" option for Step 1 to make a similar point.

Step 4

Kids who have have heard it all before might benefit from some personal testimonies that will bring to life the concept of God as the source of happiness. Ask a couple of Christians, young and old, to tell your group how they searched for happiness before they found true happiness in God. If you're feeling really gutsy, you could also invite a non-Christian to present his or her views about how to find true happiness. Encourage the group to ask questions, being sensitive to each person's beliefs. After the people have left, discuss what they had to say, especially in light of the teachings found in Scripture. Here are some passages you might use to supplement your discussion: Proverbs 14:12; Romans 15:13; I Peter 1:3-9.

Step 4

Since this whole session is based on one powerful psalm, you may want to explain the psalm in more detail. It begins with an invitation to anyone and everyone ("all the earth") to have a relationship with God (vs. 1). People who know and love God can be joyful because they have a relationship with the awesome God (vs. 2). It identifies God as Lord (vs. 3). Verse 3 tells us that there are three parts to our relationship with Him: He created us, we belong to Him, and He guides us (like a shepherd). We should praise Him (vs. 4) because He is good, He loves us, and He is faithful to us (vs. 5).

Step 5

If your group is small, assign the following questions and Scripture passages to individuals; otherwise, have kids work in pairs or small groups.
(1) What are some things we should be joyful about?
• **Luke 2:10** (The Savior's birth.)
• **Acts 17:18** (Christ's resurrection.)
• **James 1:2** (Suffering.)
• **I Peter 1:3-9** (New birth, an inheritance, salvation, eternal life.)
(2) Where does joy come from?
• **Galatians 5:22** (The Holy Spirit.)
• **Psalm 16:11** (God.)
(3) How did people in the Bible express their happiness?
• **II Samuel 6:14, 15** (David danced before the Lord; Israel shouted and blew trumpets.)
• **Acts 16:25** (Paul sang.)
(4) What brings joy?
• **John 15:10, 11** (Obeying God.)

Step 4

Rather than just discussing Psalm 100, have students sing it. There are several different versions. Choose one your kids know, or have them make up their own tune (or change/rearrange some of the words to make the psalm fit a familiar tune). They can also add a clapping pattern and/or gestures to enhance the presentation. Kids can work as one group or in small groups. (Or you might have kids individually write and present their own versions of Psalm 100 based on their personal feelings about God.) Let volunteers present their songs or readings. Follow up with prayer. Remind kids that when they worship God this way, it encourages them to focus on Him instead of on themselves.

Step 5

Have each group member write out a Bible verse about joy or happiness on a small slip of paper. (You'll probably want to have some concordances on hand for this activity.) Encourage kids to pick verses they especially like. Then have them sit in a circle. Create a more worshipful atmosphere by darkening the room and lighting enough candles to make it possible for kids to read their verses. Have each group member finish both of these sentences aloud:
• "I am really happy when . . ."
• "I would be really happy if . . ."
After each group member finishes, have the person to his or her right read aloud the verse he or she wrote down. Afterward, ask some of the kids how likely it is that they will get what they wished for and how long they think it would make them happy.

Step 4

Have group members form teams. Give each team one (or more) of the phrases from Psalm 100 that includes an action word (shout, worship, come, know, enter, give, and praise). Ask the members of each team to talk together about how our knowledge of and relationship to God contribute to helping us feel better. Then have each team plan a two-minute (or shorter) skit. In the skit, one team member should play a person needing help. The rest of the team members should then act out what they might say or do to help that person (based on the principles from Psalm 100).

Step 5

Spend some time talking in more detail about "bad" moods. Ask: **Does it make you angry when someone—especially a parent—asks you to snap out of your bad mood as if it were something you can turn on or off? What do you usually do in response? What would be a better way for someone to ask you to try to stop being so grouchy?**

If it's appropriate for your group, you might want to take some time to discuss how a woman's menstrual cycle affects her emotions. Invite some mature Christian women to share about this with the girls in your group. Be especially sensitive to the different stages your girls are in. Here are some questions you might use to get the discussion going:
• **How do your emotions change around your period?**
• **Do you think women blame too much on PMS? Why or why not?**
• **What do you do to control your emotions during your period? What have you found helpful?**

Step 4

Instead of having your guys write letters to cheer up their friends, have them just explain what they would say to those friends. If guys complain that the situation you describe is too vague, invite them to describe a real friend's problem (without naming names).

Step 5

Guys may be less willing than girls to acknowledge their down times or to talk about what they do to cheer themselves up. That's why this session does not specifically ask them if they ever feel down. Instead, it is assumes that they sometimes feel down, which takes the pressure off. No one has to be the first to admit that he gets depressed or to identify what depresses him. Encourage group members to be honest when they write down what they do to cheer themselves up. Explain that their comments will remain anonymous and that they can spread out around the room for a little privacy while they write.

Another way to address the subject is to have guys discuss positive and negative ways to use each of the following things when you're feeling down:
• music
• television or movies
• friends
• religion
• sports or exercise
• food

Step 1

Divide the group into two or more teams. Line the teams up for a relay race. (You'll need a large room for this activity.) Place baseball bats at the opposite end of the room, one bat per team. Each player has a choice when his or her turn comes. He or she may (1) run the perimeter of the room or (2) run to the bat, put his or her forehead on the tip of the bat, and circle it ten times, keeping the bat perpendicular to and touching the ground at all times. After the completing the activity of his or her choice, the player will run back to the team and tag the next person in line, who will continue the relay. The first team to have all of its members complete the relay wins. Afterward, ask kids how they chose which relay to run. If some say that they thought the bat relay would be quicker than running the perimeter of the room, point out that what appears to be the faster way may not always be the best. Follow up with the last paragraph in Step 1.

Step 3

After kids answer your questions in Step 3, have them form teams for a relay. Mark straight paths across the room with masking tape, one path per team. Give each team a pencil and a lemon. Each person on the team is to take a turn rolling the lemon across the room and back on the path, using only the pencil. If the lemon rolls beyond the masking tape, the player must start over. When the last player rolls the lemon back to the team, the first player must skin the lemon, eat it, and have an empty mouth upon inspection. The first team to do all of this is the winner. Use the sour expressions of the lemon eaters to lead into a discussion of how God can turn our sorrow into joy. Explain that you are going to read a joyful psalm. Ask: **Do you think any of our lemon eaters would be capable of writing a happy psalm right now?**

Step 1

Play a few video clips from concerts that show an audience expressing its appreciation for a performance. Start with a tame audience, one that is politely clapping. Then show an audience that is a little more lively. Finally, show an audience going crazy—clapping, cheering, whistling, screaming, and dancing. Draw parallels between these audiences and levels of happiness. Point out that God can give us different kinds of joy—a quiet, calm joy; a hearty-laugh kind of joy; and an intense joy. Explain that true, lasting joy comes only from God. Any other source of happiness is short-lived.

Step 5

Check out a couple of secular books at your local library on finding happiness. Use them to gather a variety of brief quotes that you can read and discuss with your kids. Ask: **How does this person define happiness? What does this person say is the source of happiness? How is this person's view on happiness different from what is taught in the Bible?** Actually bringing the books to the session, showing kids the covers, and reading quotes directly from the books will help to spark interest in the discussion. Then follow up with the rest of Step 5 as written.

Step 3

You can save a little time by skipping the first part of Step 3. Say: **Some people try to gain happiness by doing things that only harm them in the end. Can you think of some examples of this?** (Alcohol, drugs, sex, the pursuit of money or material possessions, power, etc.). Then ask: **Can these things really make a person happy?**

Step 4

If you're short on time, you can skip the letter-writing activity at the end of this step and move right into Step 5. The activity in Step 5 will help your kids personally apply what they've learned. Therefore, they won't miss out on application even if they skip the activity at the end of Step 4.

Step 2

After the ingredient-tasting activity, say: **Just as there are many bad-tasting ingredients in good-tasting cookies, there are bad characteristics in us and bad situations we encounter, all of which God can use to make us into better and stronger people.** Ask group members to name some other bad-tasting ingredients in good-tasting foods. Then have the group read together James 1:2-4, 12; Mark 9:49; and I Corinthians 10:13. As you discuss the passages, point out that a good chef is an expert at mixing ingredients that might not be too tasty on their own. Then suggest that Jesus is our master chef, the one who can positively blend the most negative ingredients of our personality and cook them at the right temperature in the oven of life to make us into beautiful examples of His expertise.

Step 4

Point out that all of us at times get depressed and "down." Then use the following activity to illustrate the help we all need to give each other during such times. First, get a thin volunteer and a strong volunteer. The thin one should lie on the floor; the strong one should pick him or her up. Next, try having someone a little heavier lie on the floor. It might take two persons to lift him or her. Then get two heavy people to link arms and lie on the floor. It should take several people to lift them. Point out that the heavier our problem is, or the deeper our depression, the more personal help we need to get back on our feet.

Step 2

One way to encourage camaraderie is to have small mixed groups of junior highers and high schoolers actually bake their own cookies. After the "ingredients" discussion, give the groups a couple of basic recipes to choose from. Have each group mix up a batch of cookie dough. Let the cookies bake while you work through the next few steps. Then allow kids to enjoy the fruits of their labor at the end of the session.

Step 5

Collect the slips on which kids have anonymously written how they go about cheering themselves up. As you read them aloud, don't have kids call out whether it's a good way or bad way to cheer up. Instead, find a way to encourage junior highers to express their opinions without holding back until the high schoolers have spoken. One way is to have kids hold up plus or minus signs that they've drawn on the front and back of an index card. Give them a few seconds to think by having them hold up the cards at the same time on the count of five. Make sure kids get to express the reasons behind their opinions.

Step 3

Write the words "I am happy when I . . ." across the top of the board. Instruct your sixth graders to write their responses to the statement. Collect the responses and read some of them aloud. Then ask group members to name some of the "artificial ingredients" used by kids they know to try to obtain happiness. Help kids focus on the artificial things that are a part of their immediate world. Ask: **In addition to using substances and possessions, how do we use words and actions as artificial means to happiness?** As an example, talk about how we use words to put someone else down so we can feel better about ourselves or look better in front of other people.

Step 4

After your sixth graders have talked about Psalm 100 and its helpful instructions, discuss the choices we have concerning our emotions. Say: **Although we can't choose when or how we will have an emotional response to something, what are some choices we do have? Is staying in a bad mood a choice you make or do you *have* to stay that way until it wears off? What about a good mood?** Ask kids to think of times when they felt sad, glad, or angry—without having had anything happen to make them feel that way. Ask: **When you realized that nothing had happened to cause you to feel that way, what did you do?**

Date Used:

Approx.
Time

**Step 1: Always Read
the Instructions**   _____
o Extra Action
o Large Group
o Heard It All Before
o Extra Fun
o Media
Things needed:

Step 2: Cookie Time   _____
o Small Group
o Urban
o Combined Junior High/High School
Things needed:

**Step 3: Shortcuts and
Artificial Ingredients**   _____
o Extra Fun
o Short Meeting Time
o Sixth Grade
Things needed:

Step 4: Real Happiness   _____
o Extra Action
o Small Group
o Large Group
o Heard It All Before
o Little Bible Background
o Fellowship & Worship
o Mostly Girls
o Mostly Guys
o Short Meeting Time
o Urban
o Sixth Grade
Things needed:

**Step 5: Feel-Better
Remedies**   _____
o Little Bible Background
o Fellowship & Worship
o Mostly Girls
o Mostly Guys
o Media
o Combined Junior High/High School
Things needed:

5 Emotions out of Control

YOUR GOALS FOR THIS SESSION:

Choose one or more

☐ To help kids recognize that talking to another person can often help us feel better when we're experiencing emotional turmoil.

☐ To help kids understand how to help people who are experiencing emotional turmoil—and how to ask for help from others when they are experiencing emotional turmoil.

☐ To help kids choose God as a "cord of strength" in their emotional lives.

☐ Other _____

Your Bible Base:

Psalm 139:1-5
Ecclesiastes 4:7-12

Let's Work Together

(Needed: Two strips of cloth, a spoon, several large marshmallows, a stopwatch, chalkboard and chalk or newsprint and marker [optional])

Have group members form pairs. Suggest that they pair up with people who are about as tall as they are. Explain that the pairs will be competing in a "three-legged race." The member of each pair will race to a designated point (perhaps the far wall of your meeting area) and back—with their legs tied together.

Have the pairs line up behind a start/finish line. Have the members of the first pair stand side-by-side while you tie their inner legs together. Tie one strip of cloth just above their knees and one strip around their ankles.

Just before you tell the first pair to go, introduce a twist to the contest. Give the members of the pair a spoon with a marshmallow on it. Explain that both members of the pair have to hold on to the spoon and keep the marshmallow from falling off as they race. If the marshmallow falls off, they must stop, pick it up (without falling over), set it back on the spoon, and then continue racing.

You'll need a stopwatch to time the pairs as they race. To make things more "official," you might want to write the times on the board.

After all of the pairs have taken a turn, lead the group in a round of applause for the pair with the fastest time.

Afterward, ask: **What was the key to doing well in this activity?** (Working together and communicating well with your partner.)

What are some other things that require the help of another person? (Lifting a heavy object, moving furniture, playing doubles in tennis, etc.)

If no one mentions it, ask: **What about dealing with our emotions? Does that ever require the help of someone else?** Get responses from as many group members as possible.

With a Little Help from My Friends

(Needed: Copies of Repro Resource 6, pencils)

Distribute copies of "Help Needed—or Not?" (Repro Resource 6) and pencils. Give group members a few minutes to complete the sheet.

When everyone is finished, go through the situations one at a time. Read each situation aloud and have group members hold up one or two fingers to indicate their responses. Then ask volunteers to explain why they responded as they did.

Use the following information to supplement group members' responses.

(1) *Alec just found out he made the school basketball team. He's so excited, he can barely talk.* (Alec could certainly "work out" his happiness on his own, but it would probably be much more enjoyable for him to have someone to share his joy with.)

(2) *Janna's been having weird dreams about being attacked by a stranger. As a result, she's afraid to go anywhere by herself.* (Janna needs someone to share her fears with. She's being "crippled" by her fears if they prevent her from doing normal things.)

(3) *Candy was dumped by her boyfriend two days ago. Now every time she sees him in the hallway at school, she runs to the bathroom and cries.* (Candy eventually may be able to work through her sadness by herself; but having someone to comfort and reassure her would probably speed up the process.)

(4) *Li is really moody. One minute he might be laughing and joking; the next minute he might be yelling at someone for some minor thing. Sometimes he's exciting and fun to be with; other times he's sad and depressing.* (Sudden mood swings may be a symptom of some deeper emotional—or perhaps even physical—problem. Li needs help with his situation.)

(5) *Jeff's been extremely angry since he found out his mother and father are divorcing. He's been getting into fights at school. He yells at his teachers. And he's had a couple of run-ins with the police for vandalism.* (Jeff's anti-social behavior is probably the result of his anger over his parents' divorce. Jeff needs help in dealing with his anger more effectively.)

(6) *Gabrielle made the cheerleading team; Tara didn't. Tara got jealous and started spreading lies about Gabrielle to "get even" with her.* (It's possible that Tara could work through her jealousy on her own. However, having someone to talk to about her jealousy could speed up the healing process.)

OPTIONS

EXTRA ACTION

HEARD IT ALL BEFORE

MOSTLY GIRLS

MOSTLY GUYS

SHORT MEETING TIME

URBAN

JR.HIGH HIGH SCHOOL COMBINED

SIXTH GRADE

(7) Chenelle is mad at her parents for not letting her go to a concert with her friends. She hasn't spoken to her mom or dad for two days. (It's probably safe to say that Chenelle's relationship with her parents would gradually get back to normal after a few days. However, if Chenelle had someone to talk to about her feelings, it might help clear up the situation for her.)

(8) Gary just found out he and his family are moving to another state. Gary will have to leave behind all of his friends. He's really sad about it. (Gary may be able to work through his sadness on his own. However, not having someone to talk to about his sadness may make the transition very difficult for Gary.)

(9) Last week, Alejandro found out that he has to give a ten-minute speech in front of his English class. Alejandro is afraid of speaking in front of an audience. He hasn't been able to sleep for the past two nights because he's so worried about the speech. (Alejandro may feel better sharing his fears with someone he trusts. Other people also may be able to encourage Alejandro and give him tips for easing his nervousness in front of a crowd.)

(10) At school, Eddie was always being picked on or made fun of. It made him angry, but Eddie usually didn't do anything about it. However, one day when Jeff tripped him in the hallway, Eddie's rage exploded. He jumped up, punched Jeff in the face, and then started kicking him when Jeff fell to the ground. When a couple of girls started yelling at him to stop, Eddie threw his books at them as hard as he could. After a minute or two, Eddie sat down in the middle of the hallway and started crying. (Anytime a person's pent-up anger leads to violence or rage, he or she needs help.)

Ask: **Why do we need other people's help for something as personal and private as our emotions?** (Some emotions are so big and so overpowering that it takes more than one person to handle them. Emotions can cloud our judgment; other people can give us a fresh perspective and help us see things in a new light.)

STEP

3

A Helping Hand — make three copies

(Needed: Copies of Repro Resource 7, copies of Repro Resource 8 [optional])

Say: **OK, we've seen that sometimes we may need help from others in dealing with our emotions. By the same**

token, we may also <u>need to help others deal with their emo-</u>tions. But how do we do that?

Have group members form three teams. Before the session, you'll need to cut apart a copy of "Emotional Dilemmas" (Repro Resource 7). Distribute one section to each team.

Give the teams a few minutes to read their assigned situations and come up with ideas for how they could offer emotional assistance to the people in the situations.

Use the following questions and information to guide your discussion of the activity.

Situation #1

What emotions are Kelly and Jay probably experiencing? (Sadness, anger, jealousy, depression, fear, loneliness.)

How could you help Kelly and Jay deal with their emotions? (Encourage them to talk honestly about how they're feeling; listen to them and ask questions to let them know that you really care about what they're feeling; invite them [separately, of course] to do things to take their minds off each other; avoid acting embarrassed or uncomfortable if they share their innermost feelings; calm their fears by reassuring them of their attractiveness; etc.)

If you were Kelly or Jay, what kind of help would you want from your friends as you dealt with this situation? Encourage several group members to respond.

Situation #2

What emotions is John probably experiencing? (Anger, sadness, fear.)

How could you help John deal with his emotions? (Let him know that you're always willing to talk or listen to him if he needs you; call him frequently to let him know you're thinking about him; invite him to do things with you so that he can get away from his parents occasionally; etc.) If no one mentions it, point out that this situation may require the help of a professional counselor. Part of helping John may involve encouraging him to talk to your youth leader or pastor about his situation. [You'll address the subject of professional help a little later in the session.]

If you were John, what kind of help would you want from your friends as you dealt with this situation? Encourage group members to be honest here. If they would want to be left alone by their friends in this situation, they should say so.

Situation #3

What emotions is Susan probably experiencing? (Depression, sadness, boredom.)

How could you help Susan deal with her emotions? (Encourage her to continue sharing her feelings with you; let her know you're concerned about her; affirm her as often as possible; etc.) If no one mentions it, point out that this situation *definitely* requires the help of a

O P T I O N S

SMALL GROUP

LITTLE BIBLE BACKGROUND

MOSTLY GUYS

EXTRA FUN

MEDIA

SHORT MEETING TIME

URBAN

JR. HIGH / HIGH SCHOOL COMBINED

professional counselor. You would need to encourage Susan to talk to your youth leader or pastor about her situation. If she refused, *you* would need to talk to a professional about Susan's situation.

If you were Susan, what kind of help would you want from your friends as you dealt with this situation? Encourage several group members to respond.

Explain: **John's and Susan's situations were a little different from Kelly and Jay's. John's and Susan's situations require the help of a professional counselor. What kinds of emotional situations require professional help?** (Suicidal or self-destructive behavior, violence toward others, wild mood swings, prolonged depression, family abuse problems, etc.)

If you or someone you know needed professional help, what could you do? (Talk to a trusted adult—whether it's your parents, your youth leader, your pastor, a school counselor, or someone else.)

True or false: Needing help with your emotions is a sign of weakness. (False!) Make sure your group members understand that *everyone* feels overwhelmed by his or her emotions at one time or another.

[Note: We've included "Counseling Q & A" (Repro Resource 8) as an additional resource you might want to use. If you think some group members might benefit from professional counseling, hand out the sheet and briefly review it, or let kids read it on their own. This is a serious subject, and it's hard to do it justice in the short space we have here. The point is for you to open the door for those who might be in serious need of some help. We'll trust your judgment as to whether the information on the sheet is or isn't appropriate for your group.]

STEP
4

Three Strands

(Needed: Bibles, a roll of narrow masking tape, chalkboard and chalk or newsprint and marker)

Say: **Think about one person you would turn to when you need help with your emotions. What qualities does he or she have?** Among the qualities group members might mention are being a good listener, someone who knows you well, someone you can trust, someone you feel comfortable talking to, etc.

Have someone read aloud Psalm 139:1-5. Then ask: **Who is being described in this passage?** (God.)

Point out that God is a good listener, He knows us well, and He's trustworthy. In other words, He's the perfect person to go to when we experience emotional turmoil.

How could God help us when our emotions get the better of us? (He might provide a calmness in our lives in the midst of our emotional upheaval. He might help us find a relevant passage of Scripture that gives us advice for dealing with our emotions. But perhaps the most likely thing He would do is provide someone here on earth for us to talk to about our situation.)

Have your group members read aloud Ecclesiastes 4:7-12 together. Then ask for a volunteer to come to the front of the room to help you illustrate the principle of the passage.

Have the volunteer sit in a chair facing the group. Ask the person to put his or her palms together. Wrap his or her hands once with masking tape.

Say: **A cord of one strand—someone who tries to handle his or her emotions alone—is easily broken.** Ask the volunteer to pull apart his or her hands. The tape should break quite easily.

Wrap the person's hands with two layers of tape. Make sure you wrap the second layer directly on top of the first layer.

Say: **A cord of two strands—someone who asks for help from a friend or a professional in handling tough emotional situations—is a lot stronger than a cord of one strand.** Ask the volunteer to pull apart his or her hands. The tape should be stronger, but still should be able to be broken.

Wrap the person's hands with three layers of tape. Make sure you wrap each layer directly on top of the previous one.

Say: **A cord of three strands—someone who trusts God to bring other people into his or her life to handle tough emotional situations—is virtually unbreakable.** Ask the volunteer to pull apart his or her hands. He or she should not be able to.

Explain: **God *wants* to be a cord of strength in our lives. He is always available when we ask for His help. Think about an emotion or situation that you're having problems with. Ask God for His strength and help in dealing with the situation. Ask Him to be the cord of strength in your life and in this situation.**

Give group members a few minutes to pray silently; then close the session by praying aloud.

OPTIONS

LARGE GROUP

HEARD IT ALL BEFORE

LITTLE BIBLE BACKGROUND

FELLOWSHIP & WORSHIP

MOSTLY GIRLS

MEDIA

SIXTH GRADE

Help Needed—or Not?

Read each of the following situations. If you think the situation is something the person could work out alone, write "1" in the blank. If you think the situation is something that might require the help of another person, write "2" in the blank.

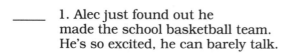

_____ 1. Alec just found out he made the school basketball team. He's so excited, he can barely talk.

_____ 2. Janna's been having weird dreams about being attacked by a stranger. As a result, she's afraid to go anywhere by herself.

_____ 3. Candy was dumped by her boyfriend two days ago. Now every time she sees him in the hallway at school, she runs to the bathroom and cries.

_____ 4. Li is really moody. One minute he might be laughing and joking; the next minute he might be yelling at someone for some minor thing. Sometimes he's exciting and fun to be with; other times he's sad and depressing.

_____ 5. Jeff's been extremely angry since he found out his mother and father are divorcing. He's been getting into fights at school. He yells at his teachers. And he's had a couple of run-ins with the police for vandalism.

_____ 6. Gabrielle made the cheerleading team; Tara didn't. Tara got jealous and started spreading lies about Gabrielle to "get even" with her.

_____ 7. Chenelle is mad at her parents for not letting her go to a concert with her friends. She hasn't spoken to her mom or dad for two days.

_____ 8. Gary just found out he and his family are moving to another state. Gary will have to leave behind all of his friends. He's really sad about it.

_____ 9. Last week, Alejandro found out that he has to give a ten-minute speech in front of his English class. Alejandro is afraid of speaking in front of an audience. He hasn't been able to sleep for the past two nights because he's so worried about the speech.

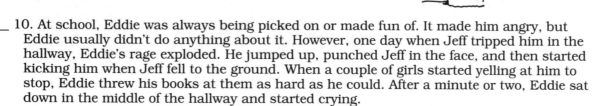

UM... ER... HUH...

_____ 10. At school, Eddie was always being picked on or made fun of. It made him angry, but Eddie usually didn't do anything about it. However, one day when Jeff tripped him in the hallway, Eddie's rage exploded. He jumped up, punched Jeff in the face, and then started kicking him when Jeff fell to the ground. When a couple of girls started yelling at him to stop, Eddie threw his books at them as hard as he could. After a minute or two, Eddie sat down in the middle of the hallway and started crying.

Emotional Dilemmas

SITUATION #1

Jay and Kelly had been going together for almost a year. They were one of the most popular couples in school. Their relationship was really starting to get serious. Unfortunately, Kelly's parents thought the relationship was getting *too* serious. They made Kelly break up with Jay.

Now Kelly and Jay aren't allowed to see each other at all. At school, Kelly's not allowed to sit with Jay at lunch or even talk to him in the halls.

You're friends with both Kelly and Jay; you've seen the emotional turmoil they've both been going through since the break-up. Kelly is obeying her parents' demands, but she's very angry with her parents. She also cries a lot at school—especially when she sees Jay talking to other girls. Jay, on the other hand, is angry at Kelly for "choosing her parents over him." He mopes around a lot and certainly isn't the fun guy he used to be.

SITUATION #2

John's parents have always fought a lot. When you used to stop by his house after school, you could usually hear his parents yelling at each other in their bedroom. But things have gotten a lot worse lately. John has hinted that his mother and father may be hitting each other.

John doesn't talk much about his parents anymore. In fact, he doesn't talk much at all anymore. He seems angry and irritable.

The last time you went over to his house, he met you at the front door. "I don't want to stay here," he said. "Let's go over to your house."

When you tried to ask him what was going on with his parents, he exploded. "Can we just drop it, please?" he said. "Just forget about my parents! It's my business and I'll deal with it myself!"

SITUATION #3

Susan, the girl who sits next to you in English class, is usually pretty quiet. But lately she's been talking to you a lot. She asks weird questions—things like "Are you afraid of dying?" and "Do you think anyone would miss you if you died?"

She also talks about how much of a pain it is to get up in the morning and face another day. She's always seemed sad and depressed, but her mood has gotten even darker in the past couple of weeks. You're afraid she might be considering suicide—but you're not absolutely sure.

COUNSELING Q & A

Many people struggle with tough issues—things like drug or alcohol addiction, eating disorders, sexual addiction, homosexuality, physical or sexual abuse, unwanted pregnancy, and suicide. All of us can benefit from the counsel of others, but those with special needs should consider formal counseling. Here are some questions people might ask about counseling:

1. What should I do first? After praying about it, seek out a trusted Christian adult (perhaps a youth worker, pastor, or school counselor) to talk to. Be very honest with this person about your struggles, and trust this person to help you. Maybe that person can counsel you, or perhaps he or she can refer you to a professional.

2. When should I seek help? It's best to seek help right away, especially if you can relate to any of these signs of danger: sense of losing control of your life, loss of interest in activities, withdrawal from friends and family, depression, too little (or too much) sleep, loss of appetite, poor school performance, aggressive or violent behavior.

3. Will counseling solve my problems? No, but it can help. Ultimately, only God can meet your deepest needs, but a counselor can help get you to the point where you can better face your situation.

4. Should I see a Christian counselor? Again, it's best to start by talking with a trusted Christian adult. You can then explore your options together, basing future counseling requirements on your particular needs, and people that are available to help.

5. What if I can't afford it? Financial concerns should never prevent you from getting the help you need. Many professional counselors have a sliding-scale fee structure to make it more affordable. It's possible that some of the expense is covered under a parent's medical plan. Check it out.

6. If I need counseling, does that mean I'm crazy? Absolutely not—but you might be crazy *not* to seek help. Counseling is not a sign of weakness; if anything, it's healthy to get help when you need it.

7. Do my parents need to know? In most cases, it's probably best that they do know, so they can support you, and possibly get help themselves if they are contributing to your problem. So much depends on your unique situation. This is an issue you'll want to discuss with your trusted adult friend.

8. If I have a relationship with God, why get professional help? Good question. Maybe God can use the skills of a counselor to bring about some healing and growth in your life. Don't view counseling as a substitute for God, view it as one tool He gives to help us.

Step 1

Even though the three-legged race suggested in the session is active, you might want to try a less common activity that helps kids work together. Have kids form teams. Give one team ten red balloons, another team ten blue balloons, and so on. Also give each team a can of shaving cream or whipped cream and ten pennies. Place a trash can in the center of the room. Explain that no one may go within ten feet of the can. When the whistle blows, kids should squirt a little cream into each balloon, put a penny in each one, blow up the balloons, tie them off, and throw them into the trash can (from a distance of ten feet). Balloons must be inflated to a minimum size. (You may want to display a sample balloon.) To determine the winning team, dump the balloons from the trash can, separate them by color, eliminate the ones that don't meet the minimum size requirement, and count the ones that are left. The team with the most balloons wins. Afterward, have each team explain its system. Did kids work as teammates or did individuals take over?

Step 2

Cut apart the ten situations from Repro Resource 6. Put the ten slips of paper into a bag. Have someone pull one of the slips from the bag, read the situation, and act out a reaction as if he or she were alone with no one else to confide in. Then have another student come on the scene to share the first kid's burden or joy. Discuss which "scene" the kids preferred: handling a situation alone or with a friend. Do the same with as many situations as you have time for.

Step 1

Play the three-legged race with a twist if you have a small group. Rather than having group members pair up, have them stand in line next to each other. Tie their legs together, forming a multi-legged chain. Place obstacles around the room to make it more difficult for the group to move. Also, assign various disabilities to slow the group down, such as blindness, muteness, paralysis in both legs, etc. Someone in line should hold the spoon with the marshmallow on it. Instead of racing, the goal is to get past the obstacles and to the other side of the room without dropping the marshmallow. Afterward, ask kids to describe how they felt during the activity. Talk about how they had to work together and communicate despite obstacles. Follow up with the last three questions from Step 1.

Step 3

If you don't have enough kids to create three teams, work through Repro Resource 7 as a group. You might also want to work through only two of the situations instead of all three. If your group is small, you probably have a good sense as to whether any of your kids would benefit from the information on Repro Resource 8. If you think it might help some kids, distribute a copy to everyone in the group. You might even want to ask group members some of the questions on the sheet *before* passing it out. This will give you an idea of what your kids think about professional counseling.

Step 1

If your group is large, you might want to have two pairs race against each other at a time. This should make it easier to determine who the winners are. You won't have to keep track of a long list of times. If you think the race will take up more time than you're willing to give it, try this: Invite a volunteer to come forward for a ballet demonstration. Ask him or her to jump up and click his or her heels together five times before hitting the ground. After a few attempts, invite two other volunteers (preferably two of your stronger group members) to come forward and assist the person. Now see if the person can click his or her heels together five times. It should be simple, if the two volunteers hold him or her up. Use this activity to lead into the questions at the end of Step 1 about relying on other people to help us work through our emotions.

Step 4

Instead of using the activity with masking tape, have group members form two kinds of teams—Helpers (with four members each) and Hurters (with two members each). Make sure you have an equal number of Helpers and Hurters teams. Tie the members of each Hurters team together back-to-back at the waist. Have them start at the wall opposite the Helpers. Assign one Hurters team to each Helpers team. The Hurters should try to stop the Helpers from getting to the other side of the room. The Helpers can run only when three of them are carrying a fourth teammate. The Hurters should chase the Helpers and try to tag the one that is being carried. If the person is tagged, the Helpers have to start over again. The game ends when the first Helpers team makes it across the room. Afterward, compare the strength of the larger teams of Helpers to the strength of the three cords or strands mentioned in the Ecclesiastes passage.

Step 2

Ask for five volunteers to perform some brief roleplays. Assign each volunteer one of the following roles: friend, parent, pastor, counselor, and psychiatrist. Instruct each volunteer to explain to the group why his or her character would be helpful to someone who is upset or has a problem. Volunteers should assume the roles of their characters and speak in the first person. For example, the "parent" might say: "I am a parent and I could be helpful to someone who is upset. I've raised five kids and dealt with all kinds of problems and emergencies. So I have lots of ideas, patience, and calmness to offer." Then select several of the situations from Repro Resource 6 and have the volunteers explain how their characters could help. Situations 2, 3, 4, 5, and 10 might work best for this activity.

Step 4

The following activity may help sensitize kids who have heard the principles contained in this step before. Have group members choose a word from Psalm 139:1-5. Write the word vertically on the left side of the board. Turn the word into an acronym by making each letter the first letter of a word or phrase that has to do with the session topic. Each word or phrase should deal with turning to other people for help when we experience emotional turmoil, helping others who are hurting, or choosing God as a cord of strength in our emotional lives. For example, *hand* could be used in the following way:
• Help others.
• Always be there.
• Never turn someone away.
• Don't forget to lend a hand.

Step 3

You might want to provide some additional scriptural background to encourage your kids to help others who are in need. Here some passages you might want to use:
• Luke 10:30-37 ("He went to him and bandaged his wounds. . . . Go and do likewise.")
• I Corinthians 12:27, 28 ("those able to help others")
• Ephesians 4:29 ("only what is helpful for building others up according to their needs")
• Colossians 3:12-14 ("clothe yourselves with compassion, kindness, humility, gentleness and patience"; "Bear with each other"; "put on love")
• Hebrews 13:15, 16 ("do not forget to do good and share with others")

Step 4

Why should kids who don't know God very well trust Him in tough situations? Have your group members look up Job 38. It's a long passage, but it describes an amazing God. Ask: **What amazing things does this passage say that God knows or has done?** (Among other things, He created the earth, the oceans and seas, the light, darkness, death, snow, hail, lightning, winds, rain, thunderstorms, deserts, grass, dew, ice, frost, the stars and constellations, clouds, and food.) Say: **The same great God who created the heavens and the earth and all of the secrets of science and who knows all of the things mentioned in Job 38 is the same God who gently invites people to come to Him when they are in need.** Have kids look up a couple of God's invitations: Matthew 11:25-30 and Psalm 9:9, 10.

Step 1

Have group members sit in a circle (preferably on chairs). If you know of close friends within the group, quietly ask them to sit across from each other, not next to each other. Hand a large ball of yam (or string) to someone in the circle. That person should hold on to the end of the yam and throw the ball to someone else. Each time the ball of yam is passed, the person who receives it should share an experience in which another person really helped him or her during a tough time. No one should receive the ball of yam twice. After everyone is holding on to a piece of yam, talk about how the people in your group can support each other emotionally. Discuss the emotional strength that can be created in the group. Then read aloud Romans 12:9-16 and discuss how it applies to helping one another emotionally.

Step 4

After the discussion in Step 4, have your group members create personal welcome mats from heavy-duty poster board. Provide colorful markers, scissors, paints, pieces of fabric, old magazines, etc., so that kids can get creative. Explain that the welcome mats will symbolize their willingness to help others in times of crisis. On the other side of their mats, they should symbolize their willingness to be helped by others in times of turmoil. Afterward, have kids explain the meaning of the symbols they chose. Encourage them to keep the mats in their rooms as a reminder to be available to help others, and to be willing to ask for help. Then have a time of prayer in which kids can tell God that they want to become part of His "support network." Let kids act on their prayers by pairing them up to discuss how they can make themselves available to each other for support during good times and times of crisis.

Step 2

After you've discussed the situations on "Help Needed—or Not?" (Repro Resource 6), talk about the emotions of guys and girls. Ask: **Do the guys you know have some of the same problems controlling their emotions that girls do? Is it easier for you to ask for help or to keep your emotions inside? Is it easier for you to be open about your feelings or to keep them private? What about guys? What can you do to be more sensitive to the guys you know as they are learning to understand the appropriate ways to express their emotions?**

Step 4

Distribute paper and pencils. Ask your group members to vote in response to the following statements by writing "yes" or "no" on their papers. **(1) I can always tell when my emotions are out of control and whether I need help. (2) I can always tell if a friend's emotions are out of control and whether that person needs help.** Collect and tally the votes; then discuss the results. Ask: **What is your responsibility in helping someone or in getting help for someone who needs it? What is your responsibility in getting help for yourself?** Mention some specific adults who would welcome the opportunity to be of help to any of your group members (and their friends), if needed. This discussion might make a good tie-in to the information on Repro Resource 8 concerning professional counseling.

Step 2

Bring in a set of barbells. Briefly train kids on how to lift safely (using the legs, not the back). Make sure that one barbell is so heavy that no one can lift it. Let a volunteer see how far he can get in picking up the barbells one at a time, beginning with the lightest one. Let other kids try the same thing. Then have kids try to guess how many people it would take to lift the heaviest barbell two inches or so off the floor. Let a couple of volunteers attempt it. (Make sure you have spotters to help if there is a problem.) Use the activity to lead into a discussion on how important it is to be open to accepting help from others when you are struggling. Also point out that it is important to be available to help others when needed.

Step 3

Often guys are encouraged to rely on themselves and to hide their vulnerability from others. Encourage your group members to be more reliant upon others and more transparent. Add the following situation to your discussion of Repro Resource 7: **Doug goes to your church. He's kind of quiet, but seems like a nice guy. You start spending some time with him and become friends with him. He doesn't usually talk about his feelings, but you get the sense that he doesn't like himself very much. He puts himself down and always tries to change the subject when you ask him anything that's even remotely personal. One day, he opens up and says he wishes he were you because you're more outgoing, better-looking, more fun to be with, and not afraid to talk to girls. What do you say?** After discussing the situation, ask: **Why is it hard for a lot of guys to talk about their feelings? What could happen to someone who never cries? What could happen to someone who never shows weakness?**

Step 1

Have someone bring a puppy, kitten, or some other baby animal to the session. Ask the person to describe all of the ways in which he or she takes care of the animal. Then have kids brainstorm ways in which caring for an animal is similar to caring for one another. Ask how people's emotional needs differ from animals'. You could also have new parents bring their baby to the session. Have them describe all of the ways in which they take care of the baby, including some of the dangers they protect the baby from. Then, as a group, brainstorm some ways in which kids could help take care of the baby—spiritually, emotionally, socially, and even physically when necessary. Challenge them to have the same concern for everyone in the group.

Step 3

Place a dozen or so paper milk cartons on a table and number them. Fill six of them with items that stink, such as vinegar, fertilizer, rotten eggs, a cigarette butt, used cat litter, etc. Fill the other six with pleasant smelling items such as perfume, half of a lemon or orange, a sweet-smelling flower, chocolate, maple syrup, etc. Cover each carton by taping a thin sheet of paper towel over the top. This will prevent kids from seeing what is inside, but will still let the odors escape. Have kids sniff the cartons and write down their guesses as to what's inside each one. You might want to award small prizes to the kids with the most correct guesses. Afterward, have someone read aloud Philippians 4:18, 19. Explain that in this passage, the apostle Paul is thanking the Philippian church for sending gifts that met his needs. Point out that if our acts of kindness to others had an odor, they would smell pleasant to God. You might also say that our reluctance to help others might smell bad to God.

Step 3

Discuss only one of the emotional dilemmas from Repro Resource 7 so that there's time to watch clips you've recorded from TV shows and movies that show people helping others who are in need. You might show scenes of someone listening sympathetically to a troubled person, someone giving advice or first aid, someone protecting a helpless person, and/or someone calming down a distressed person. If you show several clips, you might want to add some fun to the activity by letting a volunteer try to recall and describe each scene in order—after you've shown all of the clips. If the first volunteer mentions a clip out of order, go to another volunteer. Afterward, ask kids if they've been in similar situations—as either the helper or the person being helped.

Step 4

When you're finished discussing the "cord of three strands" activity, play "When You Need Someone" from The Kry's album of the same name. The Kry is a Christian rock band with a sound that your kids should enjoy. Use the song to create a worshipful atmosphere just before you close in prayer.

Step 2

To save time, have group members work only on the first five situations from Repro Resource 6. Then ask: **When kids are having emotional problems, what do they usually do to deal with those problems? Do most kids keep quiet about them? When kids do seek someone else's help, who do they usually go to first?**

Step 3

Instead of discussing the situations from Repro Resource 7, ask the following questions: **Do you think that needing help with your emotions is a sign of weakness? If your best friend was upset, would you think he or she was weak for getting help? Is it OK to get help from a friend? A parent? Some other adult? A pastor? A counselor? A psychiatrist? A psychiatric hospital?** Make sure each group member offers his or her opinion (even if it's just by nodding his or her head) for each question. These questions could be used as an introduction to Repro Resource 8.

Step 2

Ask two people to come to the front of the room and make a tight bond by linking arms. Place a mattress or a stack of pillows or blankets behind them. Then ask for a volunteer to try to push the two over. The volunteer may or may not be successful. If he or she is unsuccessful, bring up other volunteers to try to push the two over. For the second round, make the activity more challenging by having kids try to knock down a group of three. Continue adding more people to the group until the rest of the kids give up. You could use this activity to point out that the bigger the problem we face, the more help we need to bring it down.

Step 3

Here are some additional "Emotional Dilemmas" you might use with your urban group:

Situation #1

BaeBae's mother has been out of a job for over a year. The family has very little money. Today when BaeBae got home from school, he found his mother sitting on the doorstep, crying hysterically. All of the family's furniture was piled up on the curb. They'd been evicted! Realizing what had happened, BaeBae tried to be tough, but he was devastated inside. What emotions do you think BaeBae is experiencing? How could you help him deal with those emotions?

Situation #2

Jade lives in a low-cost housing development and excels in her school. But she's constantly teased, picked on, and called names because she does so well and behaves so properly. She's fed up and wants to give in and flunk a class or go do something terrible, just so the other kids will get off her case. What emotions do you think Jade is experiencing? How could you help her deal with those emotions?

Step 2

Use the following game to create camaraderie among kids of different ages. Form teams of equal numbers of junior highers and high schoolers. Set up one limbo stick per team—low enough to the ground to make it impossible to pass under it without help. The members of each team have to work together to get each person under the stick (limbo style) without letting that person fall to the floor or touch the floor with his or her arms or hands. The first team to get everyone under properly wins. Lead into a discussion about helping each other—especially when there is great need. Include the last question from Step 2.

Step 3

When you form three teams to work on Repro Resource 7, you might want to assign Situation 1 to a group that is composed only of high schoolers. They may be more comfortable than junior highers about discussing a dating problem. The other two situations will apply as much to junior highers as to high schoolers, so assign them any way you want. If you know a high schooler or a college student who has benefited from counseling, ask him or her to share a few words with your group about the experience. This would be a great lead-in to the information on Repro Resource 8.

Step 2

After your sixth graders indicate their responses on "Help Needed—or Not?" (Repro Resource 6), have them form teams of four or five. Either assign each team a situation from the resource, or ask the teams to choose one. Have the members of each team discuss how they might respond to a friend in that situation, focusing not only on what they might say, but also on what they should *not* say. After a few minutes, have the teams share their ideas with the rest of the group.

Step 4

Read aloud Psalm 139:1-5. Then, as a group, talk about how well God knows us. Ask: **When you realize that God knows everything about you— including what you're thinking— does it help you feel more comfortable with expressing yourself— including your emotions? If you're shy about showing your emotions, what can you do? How can understanding *your* emotions help you know what to do when someone else needs your help?**

Date Used:

Approx.
Time

**Step 1: Let's Work
Together** _____
o Extra Action
o Small Group
o Large Group
o Fellowship & Worship
o Extra Fun
Things needed:

**Step 2: With a Little Help
from My Friends** _____
o Extra Action
o Heard It All Before
o Mostly Girls
o Mostly Guys
o Short Meeting Time
o Urban
o Combined Junior High/High School
o Sixth Grade
Things needed:

Step 3: A Helping Hand _____
o Small Group
o Little Bible Background
o Mostly Guys
o Extra Fun
o Media
o Short Meeting Time
o Urban
o Combined Junior High/High School
Things needed:

Step 4: Three Strands _____
o Large Group
o Heard It All Before
o Little Bible Background
o Fellowship & Worship
o Mostly Girls
o Media
o Sixth Grade
Things needed:

Custom Curriculum Critique

Please take a moment to fill out this evaluation form, rip it out, fold it, tape it, and send it back to us. This will help us continue to customize products for you. Thanks!

1. Overall, please give this *Custom Curriculum* course (*Riding Those Mood Swings*) a grade in terms of how well it worked for you. (A=excellent; B=above average; C=average; D=below average; F=failure) Circle one.

   A   B   C   D   F

2. Now assign a grade to each part of this curriculum that you used.

a. Upfront article	A	B	C	D	F	Didn't use
b. Publicity/Clip art	A	B	C	D	F	Didn't use
c. Repro Resource Sheets	A	B	C	D	F	Didn't use
d. Session 1	A	B	C	D	F	Didn't use
e. Session 2	A	B	C	D	F	Didn't use
f. Session 3	A	B	C	D	F	Didn't use
g. Session 4	A	B	C	D	F	Didn't use
h. Session 5	A	B	C	D	F	Didn't use

3. How helpful were the options?
   - ❏ Very helpful
   - ❏ Somewhat helpful
   - ❏ Not too helpful
   - ❏ Not at all helpful

4. Rate the amount of options:
   - ❏ Too many
   - ❏ About the right amount
   - ❏ Too few

5. Tell us how often you used each type of option (4=Always; 3=Sometimes; 2=Seldom; 1=Never)

	4	3	2	1
Extra Action	❏	❏	❏	❏
Combined Jr. High/High School	❏	❏	❏	❏
Urban	❏	❏	❏	❏
Small Group	❏	❏	❏	❏
Large Group	❏	❏	❏	❏
Extra Fun	❏	❏	❏	❏
Heard It All Before	❏	❏	❏	❏
Little Bible Background	❏	❏	❏	❏
Short Meeting Time	❏	❏	❏	❏
Fellowship and Worship	❏	❏	❏	❏
Mostly Guys	❏	❏	❏	❏
Mostly Girls	❏	❏	❏	❏
Media	❏	❏	❏	❏
Extra Challenge (High School only)	❏	❏	❏	❏
Sixth Grade (Jr. High only)	❏	❏	❏	❏

6. What did you like best about this course?

7. What suggestions do you have for improving *Custom Curriculum*?

8. Other topics you'd like to see covered in this series:

9. Are you?
    ❑ Full time paid youthworker
    ❑ Part time paid youthworker
    ❑ Volunteer youthworker

10. When did you use *Custom Curriculum*?
    ❑ Sunday School   ❑ Small Group
    ❑ Youth Group   ❑ Retreat
    ❑ Other _____

11. What grades did you use it with? _____

12. How many kids used the curriculum in an average week? _____

13. What's the approximate attendance of your entire Sunday school program (Nursery through Adult)? _____

14. If you would like information on other *Custom Curriculum* courses, or other youth products from David C. Cook, please fill out the following:

Name: _____

Church Name: _____

Address: _____

_____

Phone: (____) _____

Thank you!